CAMBRIDGE MUSIC HANDBOOKS

Tippett: A Child of Our Time

Michael Tippett's oratorio *A Child of Our Time* was written at the beginning of the second world war as an expression of 'man's inhumanity to man'. It has become one of his most widely known works and one which is seen to symbolise the composer's extra-musical concerns, both political and psychological. This study places these concerns within a wider historical and cultural context while also focusing on specific aspects of Tippett's musical language. Central to this enquiry is Tippett's relationship to the work of T. S. Eliot, a relationship which is seen to condition both the text and its musical representation through Tippett's allusions to specific poetic images within the text and references to historical genres, forms and gestures within the musical dimension. Also of importance is the initial critical reception of the work, a reception which determined responses that still surround the work.

KENNETH GLOAG is a lecturer in music at Cardiff University.

CAMBRIDGE MUSIC HANDBOOKS

GENERAL EDITOR Julian Rushton

Tippett: *A Child of Our Time*

Kenneth Gloag

PUBLISHED BY THE PRESS SYNDICATE OF THE UNIVERSITY OF CAMBRIDGE
The Pitt Building, Trumpington Street, Cambridge, United Kingdom

CAMBRIDGE UNIVERSITY PRESS
The Edinburgh Building, Cambridge CB2 2RU, UK   http://www.cup.cam.ac.uk
40 West 20th Street, New York NY 10011-4211, USA   http://www.cup.org
10 Stamford Road, Oakleigh, Melbourne 3166, Australia

© Cambridge University Press 1999

First published 1999

Printed in the United Kingdom at the University Press, Cambridge

Typeset in Ehrhardt MT 10½/13pt, in QuarkXPress™   [SE]

A catalogue record for this book is available from the British Library

Library of Congress cataloguing in publication data

Gloag, Kenneth.
Tippett, A child of our time / Kenneth Gloag.
p.   cm. – (Cambridge music handbooks)
Includes bibliographical references and index.
ISBN 0 521 59228 3 (hardback) – ISBN 0 521 59753 6 (paperback)
1. Tippett, Michael, 1905 – Child of our time.   I. Title.
II. Series.
ML410.T467G56   1999
782.23–dc21   99-11596   CIP

ISBN 0 521 59228 3 hardback
ISBN 0 521 59753 6 paperback

For my parents

Acknowledgements

I would like to acknowledge the importance of Julian Rushton as editor of this book. His comments were always both useful and stimulating, but the shortcomings remain my own responsibility. I also extend my gratitude to Penny Souster, without whom this book would not have been possible, and the staff at Cambridge University Press.

I would like to thank those colleagues and students who have helped to create the friendly and pleasant working environment within which this book was written. In particular David Wyn Jones provided many helpful comments. Thanks also to Gill Jones and her staff in the music library at Cardiff University for their assistance in many different ways. I also thank Nicholas Jones for his help in the preparation of the music examples as well as his responses to various ideas concerning this music over the past three years, and Natasha Page for her careful reading of and comments on this material at crucial stages.

Music examples and reproduction of the text are © 1944 Schott & Co. Ltd, London. Reproduced by permission. The extracts from the work of T. S. Eliot are reproduced with the permission of Faber and Faber Ltd. 'Deep River' by J. Rosamond Johnson, 'Go Down Moses', 'Nobody Knows de Trouble I See (rare version)', from *The Book of American Negro Spirituals* by James Weldon Johnson and J. Rosamond Johnson. Copyright 1925, 1926 by the Viking Press, Inc. renewed 1953 by Lawrence Brown, 1953 (c) 1954 by Grace Nail Johnson and J. Rosamond Johnson. Used by permission of Viking Penguin, a division of Penguin Putnam Inc. The reproduction of Exx. 46 and 47 (i) from Ian Kemp's *Tippett: The Composer and his Music* is by permission of Oxford University Press. The extracts from the poetry of Wilfred Owen are reproduced with the permission of the Estate of Wilfred Owen and Chatto and Windus.

Note on the score

References to specific bars within the score take the following form: 100 refers to the bar at figure 100 and 100: 1 refers to the first bar after the figure etc. This numbering is based on the current edition of the score (Schott study score ED 10899, reprinted November 1993). However, older copies may feature a slight variation in No. 23, with figures 99–103 placed one bar later (figure 99 = my bar 99: 1 etc.). Where occasional reference is made to, for example, 'the sixth and seventh bars', this refers to the sixth and seventh bars of that specific numbered section of the score (for example, No. 1 Chorus).

Introduction

A Child of Our Time is now widely recognised as a significant musical and extra-musical statement, a work that reflects its own historical moment and assumes a position of importance within Tippett's general stylistic and technical development. This was the work through which his own idiosyncratic yet effective relationship to the written word first emerged (a factor that was to become integral to Tippett's subsequent identity as a composer), and, in conjunction with the Concerto for Double String Orchestra (1938–39), it represents a new level of technical confidence and maturity. Yet within this new-found confidence there remains a sense of struggle, with Tippett's efforts to unify his disparate musical and extra-musical sources into a technically and aesthetically integrated whole seeming never quite to succeed. Nevertheless, it is through this apparent failure that the true essence of the work may finally emerge: a paradox that will be clarified through the consideration of the text and its musical representation. The critical and technical issues surrounding Tippett's attempts to impose unity over such a wide range of diverse sources will be illuminated at various points in the subsequent discussion.

Prior to this point in Tippett's career his music seemed to be searching for an appropriate context and direction, in terms of both formal processes and stylistic identity. His protracted apprenticeship has received a certain degree of consideration,[1] with the struggle to construct large-scale musical forms evident in both the first String Quartet (1935, rev. 1943) and the first Piano Sonata (1938). Within these works Tippett's developing relationship to pre-existing large-scale forms and their realisation comes increasingly into focus, as does his fascination with images of musical pasts, a preoccupation that becomes central to *A Child of Our Time*. Within this work the encounter with past images is

1

realised through both Tippett's own text and its musical representation: a process that often takes the form of references to pre-existing stylistic and formal sources, with the allusions to these images becoming a defining characteristic of the work. The emergence of an understanding of the work as defined essentially through its intertextuality, through the interaction of its text with other texts, will provide a certain degree of background for this study. The concept of intertextuality has evolved through literary theory, the most accessible discussion of the concept being provided by Judith Still and Michael Worton. Following reference to the importance of Julia Kristeva's seminal writing on intertextuality, they state:

> The theory of intertextuality insists that a text (for the moment to be understood in the narrower sense) cannot exist as a hermetic or self-sufficient whole, and so does not function as a closed system. This is for two reasons. Firstly, the writer is a reader of texts (in the broadest sense) before s/he is a creator of texts, and therefore the work of art is inevitably shot through with references, quotations and influences of every kind . . .
>
> Secondly, a text is available only through some process of reading; what is produced at the moment of reading is due to the cross-fertilisation of the packaged textual material (say, a book) by all the texts which the reader brings to it.[2]

Although the second of Worton and Still's conditions has a clear applicability to the interpretation of music, it is the first possibility, that which views the text as a product of its relationship to other texts, which I wish to appropriate as a loosely defined background to the subsequent discussion.

Central to the overview of the work will be the reference to Tippett's own written comments and recollections. Tippett, more than most composers, often sought clarification and justification through the written word, although with varying degrees of success; with specific relevance to *A Child of Our Time*, however, his published comments form a valuable source of insight.

1

Background

Tippett – politics – pacifism

People come to pacifism for many reasons. My own conviction is based on the incompatibility of the acts of modern war with the concept I hold of what man is at all. That good men do these acts, I am well aware. But I hold their actions to spring from an inability or unwillingness to face the fact that modern wars debase our moral coinage to a greater degree than could be counterbalanced by political gains; so that the necessity to find other means of political struggle is absolute. That was certainly my conviction during the Second World War. My refusal to take part was thus for me inescapable, and my punishment with a relatively light term of imprisonment logical.[1]

Tippett's initial impulse to compose *A Child of Our Time* is widely understood as a reaction to an immediate historical event and a response to a more generalised predicament. However, beyond the specific circumstances of this work, Tippett was, and remained, a deeply conscious, committed composer, a figure who was always uniquely aware of his own position in relation to broader social, political and historical developments.

Throughout the 1930s Tippett's increasing awareness of the surrounding political climate had large-scale implications for both his own music and his relationship to a wider community. His understanding of the position of the composer within society first manifested itself through his involvement with amateur events at Oxted, the small town that was his home from 1929 to 1951. However, this involvement with community-based activities was gradually to take more explicitly political forms as the 1930s descended into an atmosphere of impending crisis. Tippett's increasing politicisation was accelerated through his involvement with the work-camps (a source of activity for the unemployed),

3

which allowed him to continue his interaction with amateur forces in a more politicised context. As a consequence of his participation in these activities he was invited to direct a group of unemployed musicians at Morley College. Thus began a long relationship between Tippett and the college, a relationship that would enable him to explore a diverse range of musical interests as well as providing a context for his own work.

His developing political concerns were to lead him in the direction of attempting to make specific statements through his work, the most overt example being the play *War Ramp*, which took the form of 'agitprop'. Performed in 1935, this play would seem to reflect Tippett's particular pacifist beliefs as well as his more general political concerns. The conclusion to the play's foreword sums up the nature of these concerns:

> The question we ask in this play is a serious one for us all. If the murderous weapons of war are to be forced once again into our hands, what are we going to do with them; where is the real enemy?[2]

However, although Tippett was involved with a community as well as with the attempt to fuse the political and the musical, his engagement with organised political activity was to remain somewhat problematic. *War Ramp* was performed under the auspices of the Labour League of Youth, yet it was to the politics of Trotsky that Tippett was most attracted. This attraction was to lead to his brief membership of the British Communist Party and the optimistic illusion that he could convert it to the Trotskyist agenda:

> In the mid-1930s I was persuaded by Phyl [Phyllis Kemp] to read Marx, but found Trotsky's *History of the Russian Revolution* more in tune with my thinking. Another book, John Reed's *Ten Days that shook the World* – an eyewitness account of the October Revolution by an American, which Trotsky approved – drew me in the direction of Trotskyism. I found Stalin antipathetic, inherently a tyrant. When Phyl persuaded me to join the British Communist Party, which was slavishly Stalinist, I agreed, thinking I would set about converting them to Trotskyism.[3]

This statement immediately reflects Tippett's own powerful and sincere outlook, an outlook that can at times seem excessively optimistic. It is difficult to speculate as to how close Tippett was, intellectually, to a Trotskyist ideology, but in the light of his existing and subsequent humanitarian concerns, it seems logical to suggest that he was attracted by the seemingly relative openness of the Trotskyist project, rather than engaging intellectually with theories of the 'permanent revolution' or with the pragmatic consequences of a systematic political commitment. In any event his involvement was short-lived, as was his initial desire to project his political and social concerns through his work. It is notable that up to *A Child of Our Time,* his most successful works – String Quartet No. 1, Sonata No. 1 for Piano and the Concerto for Double String Orchestra – are all instrumental works that reflect an ongoing preoccupation with 'abstract' musical forms and genres. Nevertheless, it is clear that the interaction of the political and the musical leads directly to *A Child of Our Time.* Even if Tippett's direct involvement in organised politics was to be short-lived, his profoundly held commitment to pacifism was to remain constant throughout the rest of his life.

Tippett provides his own descriptive recollection of the initial motivations for *A Child of Our Time:*

> A whole succession of ideas and events impinged on the oratorio that I now began to formulate: most important of all was the shooting of a German diplomat in Paris by a 17-year old Jewish boy, Herschel Grynspan, and the terrible pogrom against the Jews that followed. Grynspan seemed to me the protagonist of a modern passion story – not of a man-god, but of a man as such. When Paul Dienes showed me a review in *The Times Literary Supplement* of Odon Von Horvath's recently translated short novel, *Ein Kind unserer Zeit* (A Child of Our Time), I knew that here I had a title that was absolutely right. I sent for it and discovered in it another of the many scapegoats I wished to commemorate – the unnamed, deranged soldier/murderer, who sleeps on a park bench in the snow, at the end, frozen to death like a snowman. The work began to come together with the sounds of the shot itself – prophetic of the immanent gunfire of the war – and the shattering of glass in the *Kristallnacht.*[4]

However, a statement by Tippett which is more contemporary with the final work attracts attention not only to the fate of Grynspan but also to the impact made by a radio broadcast of Berlioz's *L' Enfance du Christ*:

> I don't remember precisely how a *Child of Our Time* first came into my head . . . I can remember being much affected by Grynspan's shooting of vom Rath at the German Legation in Paris in the Autumn of '38. And I remember listening, on Christmas Day of that year, to the broadcast of

Berlioz's lovely *Childhood of Christ*, and afterwards trying to think out what had become nowadays of the emotional power in the once universally accepted image of the Christ Child, a power which at one time could make all Europe bend its knee – at least for a season.[5]

However, although the tripartite shape of Berlioz's work could be seen in relation to the final outline of Tippett's oratorio, it does not function as a model in the way that Handel's *Messiah* and the Bach Passions will be seen to do. It is more in terms of providing an initial impulse, in conjunction with the Grynspan story, that it achieves a degree of significance.[6]

This convergence of events and ideas clearly has the figure of Herschel Grynspan at its centre, a figure who comes to symbolise individual tragedy subsumed within dramatically changing historical circumstances. Grynspan, a young German Jew of Polish origin, was living in Paris when, in August 1938, he was served with an expulsion order by the French authorities because he lacked the required permit for residency. After a period of being illegally concealed by relatives, he received news on 3 November from his sister informing him of his family's predicament following changing legal circumstances in Poland. In an act of frustration and protest, Grynspan went to the German Embassy in Paris and shot a German official, Ernst vom Rath. The historian Alan Bullock explains the background of mounting expectation leading towards this event, through the desire for just such a pretext, before outlining the true nature of the situation:

> The atmosphere of expectation . . . only needed an incident to produce an explosion. This was provided by the assassination of a German diplomat in Paris, vom Rath, on 7 November. The shots were fired by a seventeen-year-old Jew, Herschel Grünspan [Grynspan], in a despairing act of protest at the treatment of his parents and some fifty thousand other Polish Jews who were deported back to Poland, by the Gestapo, without notice. Grünspan's action was at once seized upon by Goebbels to create an atmosphere of crisis and tension. In a directive to all German newspapers, he instructed editors to see that the news of the attack should 'completely dominate the front page'. Comment must make clear that the attack would have the most serious consequences for the Jewish population.[7]

The response to this pretext by the Nazis was the unleashing of a pogrom, the so-called *Kristallnacht*. Tippett was to read of this event in the press, most notably the coverage in the magazine *Picture Post*, and his reaction to the horror was to lead to his interpretation from the specificity of the event to part of a generalised statement of reconciliation ('to at last be whole') in the form of a large-scale oratorio.

Tippett began the actual composition of the work on 3 September 1939, the day the war began. In his autobiography he connects the convergence of these events with a profound turning point within his own psychology. Following consideration of the at times turbulent nature of his personal identity, he states:

> This was the turning point in the therapy. Running parallel was the worrying affair of what had happened to the imaginative life out of which the music must come. If I succeeded in analysing myself totally, I might lose the music. I was also concerned about the matter of individuation – about the four sides to yourself, as Jung would have depicted them. Then, three nights before war broke out, I had the classic dream of a forced death: I was going to be strangled by four men. I accepted it – I said, 'Let what must, happen' – and realised afterwards that I had turned a corner. A kind of rebirth was now happening. I stopped writing down my dreams. Three days later, on 3 September 1939, the war began: simultaneously, I started writing the music for *A Child of Our Time*.[8]

2

The text

Tippett – T. S. Eliot – allusion

Central to the development of the work as a whole and the text in particular was Tippett's association with T. S. Eliot. During his student days Tippett had familiarised himself with Eliot's poetry, which was to become a significant preoccupation along with Eliot's critical writings, with 'Tradition and the Individual Talent' providing a profound point of contact and resulting influence on Tippett's wider cultural horizons.[1] Eliot's concern with the so-called 'dissociation of sensibility' and his interpretation of what he considered as the resulting corruption of English poetic traditions resonated with Tippett's own involvement with earlier English musical styles and forms, particularly the music of Purcell.[2]

The personal association between Tippett and Eliot began in 1937 and developed into deep discussions concerning poetry and language, with Eliot acting as unofficial tutor for Tippett's wider intellectual and aesthetic development. According to Tippett,

> It was quite by accident that I came into contact with T. S. Eliot. Yet soon he was to turn into a sort of artistic mentor . . . Although we had no professional involvement, I managed to talk to Eliot extensively then about the nature of poetry and drama: matters which were deeply occupying his own mind at that time [i.e. 1936–8]. Our talks took place later in his room at Faber and Faber's. I would indicate that I'd like to see him, and he would generally invite me to tea. At these tea-time conversations he (above all others) helped me clarify my notions of the aesthetics of theatre and opera. Unwittingly, he became my spiritual father. Sometimes he even guided my reading. For instance, it was through Eliot, later, that I came to read and identify closely with Yeats.[3]

This clarification of his notions of the aesthetics of theatre and opera would not manifest itself directly until between 1946 and 1952 and the composition of *The Midsummer Marriage*. But given this point of intellectual contact between the two figures, it comes as no surprise that Tippett, as is widely known, sought Eliot's involvement in the construction of the text for *A Child of Our Time*. However, rather than providing a text as Tippett had suggested, Eliot finally encouraged him to construct his own. Again, Tippett provides his own description of the dialogue with Eliot:

> In the early days, before the war, I must have known Eliot better than I can now recall; for when I came to write *A Child of Our Time*, I plucked up courage to ask him if he would provide a text. This he agreed to do, as long as I gave him a precise scheme of musical numbers and an exact indication of the number and kinds of words I considered necessary for each musical section . . . I put down on paper for Eliot a 'scenario' under the title 'Sketch for a Modern Oratorio' (the final title of the piece had not then appeared). Eliot considered this sketch for some weeks, and then gave me the surprising advice to write all the words myself. He felt that the sketch was already a text in embryo (as, in fact, it was), and whatever words he, Eliot, wrote would be of such greater *poetic* quality they would 'stick out a mile'. While remaining true to his belief in the primacy of the *musical* imagination in opera and oratorio, he considered the *poetically* imaginative words of a real poet to be often unnecessary.[4]

This discovery of his own ability to generate text was the starting-point for a method of working that would extend across the rest of Tippett's career.

The sketch which Tippett refers to does in fact contain the final text in embryo; many of the most striking poetic images were already in place, as was the overall form. In the essay that would accompany the eventual publication of the sketch, and to which reference has already been made, Tippett makes the following interesting comparison between the sketch and the final version:

> Comparing the sketch with the published work, it is clear that I was able to set down straightaway a musico-dramatic scheme (of three parts, each containing several numbers) which could remain unchanged.[5]

This tripartite scheme does, as Tippett suggests, remain unchanged, reflecting the influence of Handel's *Messiah*, the significance of which will come into focus within the next chapter.

The sketch as now published consists of a short section of text with explanatory and descriptive comments on the left-hand page. The first entry consists of what will become the first lines of the final version with its accompanying explanation:

Part 1

1.

This is to be a short constructed Chorus on a 'text', or two 'texts'. To last about a minute or more. Enough to set the mood of descent. The metaphor of winter and spring is perhaps a necessary one, as will be seen later.

('War broke. And now the winter of the world
with perishing great darkness closes in')

The lines given in brackets are a quotation from Wilfred Owen's poem 'The Seed', a text which has obvious resonance for the subject matter of and motivations for *A Child of Our Time*. According to Tippett, 'I joined this notion of seasons in history with personal experience concerning the "dark" and the "shadow" in Jung's terminology, and then wrote for Eliot the two texts of Chorus 1 in my own over-simple words':

The World turns on its dark side.
It is winter.[6]

Tippett goes on to discuss the construction and presentation of the sketch:

On the opposite left-hand page [see above], I explained discursively for Eliot what I needed, and quoted the lines from Wilfred Owen. I proceeded in this way for every number. I considered carefully the function of the proposed number, its duration, and so forth; invented or borrowed words that could stand as example; and wrote an explanation. Where I could think of no example, I wrote only the explanation and left the right-hand page free.[7]

What is most immediately apparent from this first example from the text and Tippett's description of the process is his relationship to existing texts ('invented or borrowed'): the reconstruction of Owen's words is

quite evident, as is his own reference to Jungian terminology, the significance of which will be clarified through the next stage of the discussion.
The reference to the poetry of Owen is sustained in the sketch for the
third number. The commentary contains another allusion to 'The Seed':

3.

This dialogue is all 'rhythmic translation'. The chorus is conceived of
here as mankind in general. The alto is still the world soul. The paradoxes
are beyond the mass of men, so they feel a sense of powerfulness before the
events (the Sept. crisis, etc.) – they feel spiritual impulses in an untem-
pered form, out of all control, as seeds before the wind. The association to
the war and the general upheaval is in Wilfred Owen's lines:

> But now the exigent winter, and the need
> Of sowings for new spring, and flesh for seed.

(Time: 1 to 2 minutes)

This more or less ends the feeling of 'the prologue in heaven', and may
need an instrumental interlude before the next singing.[8]

The use of Owen's poem as a source is realised in Tippett's own words as
'We are as seed before the wind, We are led to a great slaughter', with the
only alteration in the final version consisting of 'carried' in place of
'led'.[9] Tippett's reference to the 'the prologue in heaven' indicates an
awareness of Goethe's *Faust* as another textual source. As the composer
indicates: 'I prefaced each part (but especially Part I) with a chorus
which I considered functionally as a kind of "Prologue in Heaven" on
the lines of Goethe's *Faust*: that is, everything seen in the most general
terms in relation to the cosmos. I then proceeded inward from that
point.'[10]

The final reference to Owen's poetry comes in the sketch for No. 22:

22.

This is a solo like No. 6 in part 1.
It describes the boy caught in the outer and inner prisons of the law. He
thinks of his missed life, like Owen's dead soldier:

> Whatever hope is yours,
> Was my life also; I went hunting wild
> After the wildest beauty in the world

11

> Which lies not calm in eyes, or braided hair,
> But mocks the steady running of the hour,
> And if it grieves, grieves richlier than here.
> For by my glee might many men have laughed,
> And of my weeping something had been left,
> Which must die now.

It is very quiet in tone, warm and simple, distilling some of the 'pity of war', which Owen wished expressed.[11]

This description relates to the tenor solo (The Boy), which is, as Tippett suggests, concerned with the inner and outer struggle, with 'these prison walls', as stated in the sketch, providing a metaphor for this sense of containment, a metaphor which in the final version becomes 'Earth and sky are not for those in prison'.

The incorporation of Owen, given Tippett's concerns and the work's subject matter, is self-evidently appropriate. However, this emerging relationship between Tippett's text and other texts brings the focus back towards his association with Eliot. Within the final version of the text there are various allusions to Eliot's work. These allusions are identified by Kemp and they tend to indicate that Eliot may have had an influence, however that may be defined, which exceeded the initial suggestion that Tippett complete his own text. Before considering the wide-ranging implications of this somewhat tentative suggestion, it will be useful to consider these allusions in some detail.

The first reference to the potential importance of Eliot's work is the preface to the score, ' . . . the darkness declares the glory of light', which functions as a literary motif for the work as a whole. As Kemp indicates, this is a direct quotation from *Murder in the Cathedral*, 'Only in Thy light, and Thy glory is declared even in that which denies Thee; the darkness declares the glory of light',[12] which in turn draws on the Bible (Psalm 19, 'The heavens declare the glory of God'). This reference to the biblical source via Eliot immediately communicates the poetic, extra-musical essence of Tippett's oratorio, but it also begins to suggest that the work, in terms of both text and music, may begin to be imbued with certain wide-ranging intertextual associations and allusions.

However, within the main body of the text, the Eliot references become less self-evident. According to Kemp: 'Elsewhere, direct allusions to Eliot are few, but those that can be identified are striking.'[13] For example, the Scena from Part III of the score has enclosed within it a reference to, rather than direct quotation from, Eliot's *Ash-Wednesday*. The bass soloist states:

> Patience is born in the tension of loneliness.
> The garden lies beyond the desert.

Kemp identifies in this line a reference to a quite specific poetic image from Part V of *Ash-Wednesday*:

> In the last desert between the last blue rocks
> The desert in the garden the garden in the desert
> Of drouth, spitting from the mouth the withered apple-seed.
>
> O my people.[14]

In this instance, Tippett's reworking of Eliot's 'The desert in the garden' is indeed striking. But what also seems remarkable is Eliot's repeated cry of 'O my people', a poetic image which seems to resonate with Tippett's use of both the ambience and substance of the Negro spiritual within the musical context, a possibility which Kemp does not recognise.

The next reference which Kemp does identify comes in the General Ensemble that acts as the penultimate section of Tippett's score. The soprano sings: 'Here is no final grieving, but an abiding hope'. According to Kemp, this line is a reworking from Part I of *Murder in the Cathedral*: 'Here is no continuing city, here is no abiding stay'.[15] In Tippett's sketch for the text the commentary that accompanies the initial outline for this entry contains a direct reference to the work of Eliot, but this reference is not to *Murder in the Cathedral* but to *Gerontion*. The full entry in the sketch reads as follows:

> After the preceding *scena* there will probably be a short musical interlude to mark the 'moment of silence' before the final awareness. The tenor and soprano still stand for the distinctively human figures. When all these texts have been sung, the chorus repeats them in a swelling ensemble. We have reached the point where man must dare to know himself, cost what it may.
>
> 'After such knowledge: what forgiveness? . . .'
>
> 'Think
>
> Neither fear nor courage saves us. Unnatural vices

Are fathered by our heroism. Virtues
Are forced upon us by our impudent crimes.
These tears are shaken from the wrath-bearing tree.'[16]

Tippett's first attempt to fashion this imagery into a workable text takes the form of:

GENERAL ENSEMBLE: CHORUS AND SOLOISTS

TENOR.   I would know my dark side
and my light, so shall I at
last be whole.

BASS.   Then courage, brother, and dare the
difficult passage.

SOPRANO.   Here is no final grieving
but an abiding hope.

ALTO.   The moving waters renew the earth.
It is spring.

CHORUS REPEATS AND ENLARGES.[17]

This initial version is translated directly into the score without any significant alterations. It is at times difficult to retrace Tippett's thinking from the sketch to the score. In this instance that between the sketch and score is obvious but that between the description that accompanies the sketch and the corresponding text is more difficult to interpret. For example, the extended quotation from Eliot's *Gerontion* seems to connect only with what, in Tippett's construction, becomes images of courage and fear ('Then courage, brother, dare the grave passage').

Kemp's final example comes from the tenor solo in Part I of the score: 'I am caught between my desires and their frustrations as between the hammer and the anvil.' This line is clearly another direct reference to Part I of *Murder in the Cathedral*: 'What peace can be found to grow between the hammer and the anvil?'[18]

These allusions to Eliot's work, leaving aside the contribution they may make to the meaning of Tippett's text, indicate a degree of poetic influence. However, by shifting them from the margins of Kemp's survey into the centre of the present discourse, it is possible to suggest, as has already been tentatively indicated, that Eliot's influence on Tippett's work functions on a deeper and arguably more significant level. The allusions to Eliot, along with other literary and psychological references – Owen, Jung – begin to suggest that the text has the potential to be interpreted as a web of intertextual allusions. In other words, the text begins to define its own identity and integrity through its relationship to other texts. Tippett's allusions to Eliot begin to echo the role of allusion in Eliot's own work, and this process in turn will be carried forward into the actual musical substance of *A Child of Our Time*.

As will be clarified in chapter 3, Tippett's musical construction is based on the tripartite formal design of Handel's *Messiah*. The appropriation of the historicised model communicates a specific self-conscious reference to a past, perhaps dead, musical material; a material that is recycled, redefined, perhaps translated, into the new context. While this is not to suggest a specifically situated intertextual relationship between Tippett and Handel, this blatant revisiting of a past is clearly an integral quality of Tippett's work, a quality it shares with Eliot's poetic language.

While the difference between Tippett's appropriation of a historicised formal framework and stylistic gesture, and Eliot's recycling of a fragmented, but often precisely situated, past (most clearly evident in *The Waste Land*) must be kept in mind, there is nevertheless a shared relationship towards the inherited historical material. Within the context of Eliot this leads to fragmentary allusions, which are widely discussed and documented in the critical literature on Eliot and his work, whereas, at least on first impression, Tippett's revisitation manifests itself through the appropriation of genre and form.

However, in anticipation of the examination of the actual musical details of Tippett's score, it becomes apparent that this sense of allusion functions in a more precise sense than just the large-scale formal and generic, the most obvious being the incorporation of the Negro spiritual. Less obvious, but more significant, are the stylistic references which seem almost to exist in parenthesis. For example, Ex. 2.1 consists of the narration as sung by the bass solo in Part I of the score. The stylistic allusion to the recitative of the Baroque oratorio is quite obvious, reflecting the prevailing neoclassical aesthetic which surrounds the work. Within this example we see the parlando effect of the voice in combination with a sustained harmonic basis in the strings which, along with the initial arpeggiated chord, all combine to convey the impression of the recitative texture. In effect the passage seems to be a self-conscious anachronism.

Ex. 2.1

This could also be said of the passage that immediately follows, the 'Chorus of the Oppressed' (Ex. 2.2a). Once again the musical material is deliberately dated, with the fugal textures in the vocal parts providing a musical gesture dislocated from the extra-musical context which it is intended to portray. This discrepancy between the extra-musical 'time' (contemporary) and its musical representation (historicised) becomes, as

Ex. 2.2

(a)

(b)　　(32 : 5)

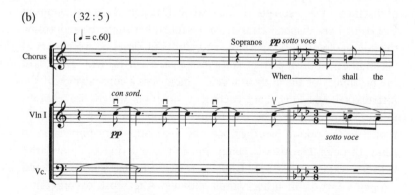

will be demonstrated through detailed discussion of the score, a recurring feature of the work.

These stylistic allusions, which provide an interpretative path through the work, combine with the intertextual allusions outlined above to construct a text which exists through its relationship to other texts, both musical and literary. As already suggested, this sense of allusion is integral to Eliot's own work. In discussing the identity and function of allusion in *The Waste Land*, a text that most clearly resonates in relation to a multiplicity of other texts, Harriet Davidson states that:

> The function of allusion in *The Waste Land* has been much debated; allusion can be considered a metaphoric device, which depends on similarities between the text alluded to and the present text. But allusion is also a dispersive figure, multiplying contexts for both the present work and the text alluded to and suggesting a cultural, historical dimension of difference.[19]

There is much in Davidson's description that could be translated into the context of Tippett. The notion of allusion as 'multiplying contexts', for example, relates to the diversity of perspectives from which we can hear specific moments and gestures in *A Child of Our Time*. But, more importantly, the notion of difference which Davidson introduces is fundamental. Tippett's purely musical allusions function through this new multiplicity of contexts in a position that is as much critical as it is repetitive in relation to the historicised point of origin. In other words, although we still see the recitative texture as symbolic of a different musical time, Tippett simultaneously reflects this and generates a sense of distance.[20] Davidson goes on to state that 'In general, the allusions in *The Waste Land* disperse clear meanings into other contexts, undermine the notion of authentic speaking, and blur boundaries between texts.'[21] Again, the relationship to *A Child of Our Time* is self-evident. The loss of the possibility of the authentic voice emerges as a consequence of the intertextual allusions, constructing a situation which has obvious musical implications (who is actually 'speaking' in Ex. 2.1?). But, to return to the notion of difference, the most important dimension to come through Davidson's comments is the blurring of boundaries between texts: where does Handel's tripartite formal schema end and Tippett's begin? In other words, although the sense of difference between the two is obvious, the positioning of the point of separation between them is blurred and therefore, although to the listener the sense of difference between the two may be quite apparent, any possibility of a sustainable binary opposition between the sound worlds of Handel and Tippett is immediately and effectively subverted.

There are other, perhaps more obvious points of convergence between the work of Tippett and Eliot. Again using *The Waste Land* as a point of comparison, it is possible to begin to hear the highly sectional-ised, juxtaposed nature of *A Child of Our Time* as another potential refl-ection of Tippett's awareness of Eliot. In any interpretation of Eliot's work, but particularly in relation to *The Waste Land* and *Four Quartets*, the disjunct, fragmentary presentation of the poetic material is immedi-ately apparent. As Jewel Spears Brooker indicates, 'The basic principle of structure in *The Waste Land* is the juxtaposition of fragments . . . The basic principle in *Four Quartets* is repetition.'[22] Fragmentation and repe-tition are two qualities which become integral to Tippett's stylistic and technical development after *A Child of Our Time*. Although within the immediate context of this work literal repetition does not always directly manifest itself as a structural and/or stylistic quality, the coincidence of texture with formal division is quite apparent, although not to the extent that it will become in some of the later works. This sense of textural dis-continuity is evident from the 'transition' between Exx. 2.1 and 2.2a, with the sustained C providing a link between the two numbers (Ex. 2.2b), but this link does not appear to be of such an integrated nature that it would allow for the two numbers to be conceived as unified through this 'transition'.

Tippett and Jung

Although the figure of Eliot remains the central reference point, Tippett's fascination with the psychology of Jung provides yet another element in the constellation that is the text. His awareness of the analyti-cal psychology of Jung has been well established. In his autobiography he describes his increasing understanding of Jung in relation to his own personal circumstances: 'Evelyn Maude had given me Jung's *Psychology of the Unconscious*, and I had become fascinated by its ways of interpret-ing dreams. Then I read more and more Jung, even the hefty volume, *Psychological Types* . . . I found that Jung had much to offer in relation to my difficulties.'[23] This statement can be interpreted as a reflection on his life during the 1930s, a period which we can see as forming an extended prelude towards the eventual realisation of *A Child of Our Time*. Given this point of potential convergence it comes as no surprise that Tippett's final text is, as already suggested, imbued with certain Jungian connota-tions.

According to David Clarke, 'the impact of Jungian ideas on his artistic output is first evidenced in *A Child of Our Time* and *The Midsummer Marriage* (1946–52), and in one way or another the Jungian themes of self-knowledge, rebirth and the reconciliation of opposites pervade his later *œuvre* with varying degrees of emphasis'.[24] Within the text Tippett's awareness of Jung manifests itself through various images that have their point of origin in Jungian terminology rather than through direct quotation or allusion. Jung's influence is felt most directly at certain passages of the initial sketch for the text. For example, the sketch for the opening chorus of Part III is accompanied by a description which is heavily dependent on Jungian imagery. Tippett describes the descending motion, which provides a correlation to the opening of Part I: ' The descent into the water is a universal dream symbol of the present day.'[25] This statement is followed by an extended direct quotation from Jung that concerns psychological images of descent and water:

> *A Protestant theologian often dreamed the same dream*: He stood on a mountain slope with a deep valley below, and in it a dark lake. He knew in the dream that something had always prevented him from approaching the lake. This time he resolved to go to the water. As he approached the shore, everything grew dark and uncanny, and a gust of wind suddenly rushed over the face of the water. He was seized by panic, fear, and awoke.
>
> *This dream shows us the natural symbolism. The dreamer descends into his own depths, and the way leads him to a mysterious water. And now there occurs the miracle of the pool of Bethesda: an angel comes down and touches the water, endowing it with healing power.*
>
> ... *We must surely go the way of the waters, which always lead downward, if we would raise up the treasure, the precious heritage of the father.*[26]

These images of water, descent and possible healing (reconciliation?) are 'translated' by Tippett into his own poetic construction. In the sketch, which is accompanied by this quotation from Jung, these images take the form of:

> Chorus.
> The cold deepens.
> The earth descends into the icy waters, for there lies the jewel of great price.

For the final version these lines remain almost exact, with the only notable change being the substitution of 'world' for 'earth':

The cold deepens.
The world descends into the icy waters,
where lies the jewel of great price.

Examples from earlier stages in the sketch provide more implicit use of Jungian imagery. For example, the commentary which accompanies the entry for the tenor solo (No. 6) provides references to the Father-God and the anima:

This is 'rhythmic translation' again.

The tenor and soprano soloists are conceived of here as the personification, humanization of the common man and woman (young). The metaphor should be homely, proletarian, warm, and human – as a foil to the abstractions of the soul and the Father-God. The man tells of his psychological split self which appears to him, and actually is on a certain plane the frustrations of his condition in the commonwealth. He has lost the relation to his soul, to the impersonal things, hence the feminine, the women have demonic power (or he has an infantile fixation, etc.). He projects the anima on his womenfolk, with devastating personal misunderstandings and complexes. But the imagery used should be entirely personal, practical, and homely, so that the ordinary man listening, still embedded in concretizations, can feel himself truly expressed and understood. Without this coming down to earth, the oratorio would fail of its purpose.[27]

This entry, which is timed at 1 to 2 minutes, resonates with psychological images ('his psychological split self') so that it becomes somewhat difficult to trace its relevance for what finally is given in the score. The first version which is presented with this extended commentary is as follows:

Tenor solo
'Starvation of body and mind is eating into my spirit.

I am caught between my desires and their frustration as between the hammer and the anvil.

Women have hold on my entrails,
how can I grow to a man's stature?'[28]

In the final version this becomes:

I have no money for my bread; I have no gift for my love.

> I am caught between my desires and their frustration as between the
> hammer and the anvil.
> How can I grow to a man's stature?

This passage has already been identified as an allusion to T. S. Eliot. It is now possible to see this line as emerging from the psychological thinking outlined in the initial commentary, with the notion of the psychological split self generating the image of being 'caught between my desires and their frustration', a binary opposition that connects with the 'hammer and the anvil'. This example provides a fascinating interface between the influences of Eliot and Jung: the intertextual process as well as some of the actual imagery involved reflects not only Tippett's awareness of Eliot but also the influence of poetic imagery which originates from within Jungian psychology.

This process of translating Jungian imagery into his 'own' context was evident in the earlier discussion of the initial sketch, along with Tippett's use of images of 'the dark' and 'the shadow', both of which are central elements in Jung's understanding of the human psyche. In discussing the importance of the image of the shadow, Anthony Stevens provides the following useful description:

> The tendency is to build acceptable traits into the persona and to keep unacceptable traits hidden or repressed. These socially undesirable aspects of the maturing personality are usually relegated to the personal unconscious, where they coalesce to form another complex, or part personality, that Jung called the shadow.
>
> Jung felt 'shadow' to be an appropriate term for this disowned subpersonality for there is inevitably something 'shady' about it, hidden away as it is in the dark lumber-room of the Freudian unconscious.[29]

These psychological images resonate throughout the work, from the initial 'The World Turns on its Dark Side . . .' to the penultimate section of the work which, as Kemp indicates,[30] provides a final affirmation of the centrality of Jung, with both the image of the shadow and the desire for reconciliation clearly indicated:

> I would know my shadow and my light,
> so shall I at last be whole.

This extra-musical, psychological image of reconciliation ('so shall I at last be whole') can be related directly to Tippett's attempt to at last make whole the diverse range of his musical and extra-musical sources. However, these disparate sources which form the basis of Tippett's text – the allusions to Eliot and Jung, the appropriation of the Negro spiritual – come together to form a loosely defined constellation without ever fully achieving an integrated identity. It is this sense of the plural and the heterodox, which within our contemporary critical context we can interpret as immensely positive qualities, that becomes the defining characteristic of the text and is carried forward into the musical dimension. That Tippett clearly conceived and perceived the work as an integrated whole, as evidenced through the Jungian desire for reconciliation, should not necessarily be seen either as constructing a conceptual boundary that automatically marginalises other competing interpretations or as providing the definitive perspective on this work.

Tippett, Eliot and the aesthetics of modernism

Through the interaction with both the figure and the work of T. S. Eliot and his attempt to reconcile the fragmentary nature of his material, Tippett projected himself against a background formed by the critical mainstream of modernism, and through his extended links with musical and literary pasts, in a somewhat circular fashion, into the context of neoclassicism: a context that had emerged in partial reaction to the radical impulses of the earlier phases of modernism and formed the prevailing aesthetic context for Tippett's early stylistic and technical development.

Eliot is widely acknowledged as the defining poetic voice of modernism. As Rainer Emig asserts, 'His poems are icons of modernism.'[31] In contrast, Tippett's relationship to modernism can be seen as somewhat problematic. According to Arnold Whittall, 'Tippett has not sought to commit himself to the "modernist mainstream": but his points of contact with it, and his highly individual refinements of, and commentaries on some of its most fundamental features are nevertheless of far-reaching significance.'[32]

Tippett's music, as suggested by Whittall, does not commit itself fully to the aesthetic and critical project of modernism. Nevertheless, there is a sense in which features such as opposition, juxtaposition and allusion in his work correspond to the experience of modernism, the most

23

important being that which becomes central in *A Child of Our Time*: the ongoing reinvention of musical pasts. This quality now brings the work alongside the prevailing neoclassical phase of modernism. Jewel Spears Brooker considers a defining characteristic of modernism to be 'the tendency to move forward by spiralling back and refiguring the past. The main literary reference point will be T. S. Eliot, whose work is paradigmatic in regard to this characteristic.'[33] This description lends itself easily to *A Child of Our Time*. Tippett's modernism, through the allusion to past styles – something which we can now see to at least have a parallel with, if not precise origins in, Eliot's poetic language – redefining this past in the light of the experience of modernism. It is through this process, as much as it is through its subject matter, that *A Child of Our Time* becomes a text of its time.[34]

3

Origins

Although many musical concerns and experiences contributed to shaping *A Child of Our Time*, Tippett clearly indicated the importance of two sources: Handel's *Messiah* and the Passions of J. S. Bach. While attention will be given to the resistance of the musical materials to Tippett's attempt to forge a sense of unity between many divergent sources, there is a basic coexistence and compatibility between the points of origin provided by the Handel and Bach models, with the Handel providing an overall sense of shape and the Bach constructing possible textures and situations within that shape.

Origins (1): Tippett and Handel

The importance of Handel's *Messiah* has already been indicated. It is now necessary to bring Tippett's relationship to that particular work more directly into focus, as it is through this relationship that Tippett was able to shape the overall design for his own work and position it in relation to the stylistic and generic conventions of the oratorio.

Tippett's initial musical starting-point for *A Child of Our Time* was a performance he prepared and conducted of *Messiah* in 1931, with amateur forces at Oxted. Many years later, writing in his autobiography, Tippett recalled this moment and its wider significance:

> One of my major projects was a complete performance (rare in those days) of Handel's *Messiah*, with the small orchestral forces for which he had written it. We spent a year rehearsing it. For me it was far more than just another concert. It was a lesson in the dramatic relationships between words and music. I was becoming clear in my mind about the distinction between what was theatrical on the stage and what was theatrical in an oratorio. I gleaned this partly from Albert Schweitzer's book on Bach, where

early on he dealt with the various modes of word-setting. The great revelation of *Messiah* was simply looking at the libretto – just to discover what Handel's starting-point had been and how he proceeded from words to music.[1]

This 'lesson in the dramatic relationships between words and music' was to be applied in *A Child of Our Time*, even though, as will be argued in the discussion of the work's early reception, this relationship is not always seen as successfully realised. Also of significance is Tippett's realisation of the distinction between the theatrical dimensions of opera and other dramatic works, a problem which emerged in earlier attempts to realise political interests within musical contexts and one which was eventually to be resolved through what Tippett saw as the essentially contemplative nature of the oratorio genre. After discussion of the details and nature of the performance, Tippett further reinforces the importance of this point of contact with *Messiah*: 'All of this was crucial to me as a composer: it certainly shaped my thinking when, later, I came to write *A Child of Our Time*.'[2]

The most fundamental aspect which Tippett was to take from *Messiah* was its tripartite formal design, which, in conjunction with the Bach Passions, the significance of which will be returned to, was to condition the overall outline of *A Child of Our Time*. Tippett provides his own accurate description of this association:

> The shape of *Messiah* is tripartite. The first part is all prophecy and preparation. The second part is epic: from the birth of Christ to the second coming, judgement, millennium, and world's end. The third part is meditative: chiefly, the words of St Paul. Incomplete performances grievously impair this wonderful shape. But I have always observed and admired it. I decided to accept this format for *A Child of Our Time*, by keeping a first part entirely general, restricting the epic material to a second part, and using a third part for consequential comment.[3]

The more specific nature of Tippett's own version of the tripartite scheme is outlined through the following description of the overall design:

> This three-part division works out for *A Child of Our Time* in the following way. Part I deals with the general state of oppression in our time; Part II presents the particular story of a young man's attempt to seek justice by

violence and the catastrophic consequences; while Part III considers the moral to be drawn, if any.[4]

Within this broad formal outline are framed the three stages of Tippett's narrative: the general, the particular and the moral. The next main element is the insertion of the spirituals at dramatically significant moments.

Origins (2): Tippett, J. S. Bach and the spiritual

Tippett's incorporation of the music and text of the spirituals into his own musical contexts is surely one of the most well-known, and perhaps most remarkable, features of the work, and it is through the positioning of the spirituals at strategic points in the design that Tippett was able to further shape the work as a whole.

It is clear from Tippett's description of the final form of the overall design and the wider considerations of the text that his primary concern was with the generalisation of the experience rather than just the specific circumstances of the Grynspan story. This concern led to a search for a generalised musical statement. From this search Tippett took as his starting point the position of the Lutheran chorale from the historical and musical context of the Bach Passions. In comparison with *Messiah*, Tippett states that

> The scheme of the Lutheran Passions is of course more unitary, based as it must be on the liturgical gospel set for Passion Sunday. Within that unitary scheme the traditional musico–verbal functions can always be distinguished: narrational recitative, descriptive chorus, contemplative aria, and finally the special Protestant constituent of the congregational hymn. I wanted to use *all* these functional practices within the tripartite shape borrowed from *Messiah*.[5]

These 'musico–verbal functions' are clearly realised in the final work. 'Narrational recitative' is an accurate description of Tippett's writing for the Narrator; in terms of both dramatic and musical function, these passages, as already mentioned in chapter 2, reflect the generic conventions of the recitative while, in terms of dramatic function, they provide the continuity within the work's narrative. The 'descriptive chorus' also has its place in the work. An extended chorus such as that which opens

Part II (No. 9), 'A star rises in mid winter', can easily be heard as 'descriptive' in that the musical realisation of the text is an accurate representation of its dramatic context. Even more relevant to the function and identity of the 'descriptive chorus' is the 'Double Chorus of Persecutors and Persecuted' (No. 11). This extended section, which is anticipated by the 'narrational recitative' of No. 10, consists of a dramatic dialogue between the two choruses, a texture which can be seen to have its origins in Bach's use of the double chorus in the *St Matthew Passion*. Tippett makes even more overt reference to the 'contemplative aria'. For example, the writing for the soprano soloist in No. 7 ('How can I cherish . . .') is both reflective and contemplative in terms of its subject matter and its realisation. Such moments of contemplation recur throughout the score, particularly in the writing for the soprano and alto soloists. However, it is the reference to 'the special Protestant constituent of the congregational hymn' which results in the most remarkable and individual aspect of the work: the utilisation of the spiritual as a parallel to the chorale in Bach's Passions.

Tippett goes on to recall the moment he became aware of the potential of the spiritual within the overall context of the work:

> one never-to-be-forgotten Sunday, I heard a singer on the radio sing the Negro spiritual 'Steal Away'. At the phrase, 'The trumpet sounds within-a my soul', I was blessed with an immediate intuition: that I was being moved by this phrase in some way beyond what the musical phrase in itself warranted. I realized that in England or America everyone would be moved in this way, forcing me to see that the unique verbal and musical metaphor for this particular function in this particular oratorio had been found.[6]

Tippett is claiming a universal significance for the spiritual, seeing it as a potent musical metaphor beyond its own immediate context, a view which now may seem somewhat optimistic but one which accentuates Tippett's concern for the generalisation of human experience. He goes on to describe the discovery of the precise source of spirituals that he would employ:

> I sent to America for a collection of spirituals, and when these came, I had an experience possibly similar to those of the Lutheran composers. I opened the collection, and found that it contained words and tunes for

every dramatic or religious situation that could be imagined. I chose five spirituals, therefore, for their tunes and words, which provided the exact 'congregational' metaphor for five calculated situations in my scheme.[7]

In his sketch for the text Tippett refers to the position of the first spiritual ('Steal away') at the conclusion of Part I as the point at which 'the oratorio reaches the modern universal musical symbol', a statement which dramatises Tippett's own understanding of the significance of the spiritual as part of a shared experience rather than a culturally specific code.[8]

By the time Tippett had presented the sketch of the text as outlined in chapter 2, he had decided on five spirituals and their position within the work:

'Steal away' (end of Part I)
'Nobody knows the trouble I see, Lord' (centre of Part II)
'Go down, Moses' (towards the end of Part II)
'O, by and by' (end of Part II)
'Deep river' (end of Part III)

The positioning of the spirituals at what Tippett describes as these 'five critical points' in the score gives a sense of focus to the overall design, with the end of each of the three parts being marked by the inclusion of a spiritual and the approximate centre of Part II being symbolically represented through the deployment of 'Nobody knows'. The description in the sketch which accompanies 'Nobody knows' describes it as 'A spiritual, describing the boy's anguish of mind and the general contemporary anguish of soul'.[9] This description indicates a certain sense of departure in comparison to that of the first spiritual, in that the emphasis on 'the boy's anguish of mind' suggests a certain specificity to the moment. However, the connection of this to 'the general contemporary anguish of soul' again reflects Tippett's concern with the interaction between the general and the specific through the context of the spiritual.

The dramatic function of the spiritual is again made explicit in the setting of 'Go down, Moses', which is described as 'A spiritual of Anger'. This sense of anger marks a stage in the development of the dramatic narrative from the 'universal musical symbol' of 'Steal away' through the 'anguish' and despair of 'Nobody knows' to this new state of anger. This sense of anger is prepared through the subject matter of the previous chorus (No. 19, The Terror) and the Narrator (No. 20, 'Men were ashamed . . .') and provides a moment of climax to this stage of the drama.

Tippett's sketch for the fourth spiritual, 'O, by and by', provides the following description:

> This spiritual describes the common human need for some spiritual certainty, for 'peace'. The way through is only dimly felt, not as yet understood. In fact there is only the awareness of the deep need and sometimes only from the unconscious, while the conscious mind persists along outworn political clichés, etc.[10]

This concern with peace and certainty provides a powerful contrast to the anger of the previous spiritual, a concern which is reflected in the relaxed musical setting of the text. The fifth and final spiritual, 'Deep river', provides what Tippett describes as 'the generalised expression of the hope of the new spring'.[11] This moment of optimism provides the last stage in a dramatic narrative which has progressed from the 'universal musical symbol' through the anguish of 'Nobody knows' and the anger of 'Go down, Moses', to the peace and certainty of 'O, by and by' and the hope of 'Deep river', a moment which can be interpreted as the final statement of the desire for reconciliation that has provided the consistent dramatic background for the work.

As well as constructing this pathway through the dramatic narrative, the five spirituals also combine to provide moments of focus and repose in contrast to the flux and fluidity of what Tippett constructs as the surrounding musical contexts to these moments. That the nature and integrity of the extent of the integration between these moments and their surrounding contexts will be raised need not detract from their importance in giving shape to both the musical and literary dimensions of the work.

4

Synopsis – analysis

The following synoptic outline provides a brief indication of the individual identity of each number. As an integral part of this process, close analytical attention will be given to certain details which emerge through the consideration of the large-scale harmonic character of each number, with specific intervallic relationships, principally the minor third and perfect fourth/fifth, providing a point of recurring reference for the analysis. The focus on these selected factors is based on the importance attached to them by Tippett himself, the specific intervals of the minor third and fifth being extracted from the context of the spirituals to construct the main source of the attempted unification of the diverse musical materials. In chapter 5 the accumulation of these details will be viewed through a wider perspective which will take as its starting point Tippett's own comments.

Part I

Part I consists of eight distinct and clearly demarcated numbers with an interludium providing a point of connection between the second and third. Each number features its own unique texture as well as harmonic identity, often standing in a somewhat disjunct relationship to its surrounding contexts.

1. Chorus

The world turns on its dark side.
It is winter.

The initial orchestral texture reflects the extra-musical image of descent, with the chromatically descending bass line moving from the opening C♯ to a point of arrival on E in bar 0: 6. This motion is covered by the E minor sonority in the trombone parts, which then initiates its own descending motion, arriving on the dyad formed between C and E in bar 0: 5. The arrival of the bass on E at this point (0: 6) connects with the initial E minor triad to present this harmony as the initial pitch centre for the work. However, although at this stage the focus on this pitch is quite explicit, the remainder of this opening number will question its importance. E takes on melodic significance from bars 0: 5/6, with the rising minor third figure from E to G in the violin 1 part again drawing attention to the former's centrality. The music moves away from E with a bass line which seems to lack direction but which eventually leads towards the clarification of B. The arrival of the string texture on B and the vertical realisation of the B major harmony is followed by a general pause; the immediate silence creates an added sense of focus on this moment (bars 1: 6, 1: 7) before the ensuing instability of bars 1: 8 to 2: 5. This point of arrival on B is also of significance as the first indication of a shift from E to B, establishing a process of juxtaposition between these two pitches which will define the textural and structural character of this opening number.

The first entry of the choral parts at bar 2: 6 is preceded by further chromatic motion in the lower strings which provides a parallel to the first six bars. The first choral entry is built on the sustained B as a harmonic pedal effect. Above this harmonically static texture a sense of momentum is developed through the quasi-imitative texture of the choral entries:

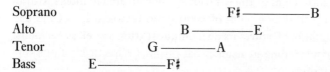

```
Soprano                              F♯————————B
Alto                      B————————E
Tenor            G————————A
Bass    E————————F♯
```

The texture moves towards bars 3: 7 – 3: 9, with the 'dark side' of the text being represented through a vertical sonority on 'dark' built upon the minor third (see Ex. 4.9a). The 'diminished' quality which results from this accumulation of minor thirds (D–F–A♭), with one major third (A♭–C), produces an effective musical realisation of the text, but one which, in pursuing such a predictable gesture, also reflects Tippett's indebtedness to inherited conventions and models. This moment is given added importance through the process of convergence towards it, with step-wise descending motions towards the minor thirds formed between C and E♭ and G and B♭:

Soprano	C ——————— B♭
Alto	F ——————————— E♭
Tenor	D ——————— C
Bass	A♭ ——————— G

The melodic/thematic potential of the minor third has already been indicated (see bars 0: 5/6); now it is given added musico-dramatic significance through its vertical realisation at this crucial juncture in relation to the text.

The rising minor third outlined at bars 0: 5/6 returns at bars 4: 2/3, but now transposed so that it is formed through a rise from F to A♭. This moment provides the first indication of the potential significance of such repetitions of the recurring interval through transposition. This repetition continues with the initial choral texture returning at bar 4: 6 but now the static pedal is provided by E. Again, in contrast to the centrality of E, F♯ is realised as a vertical sonority at bar 6: 8, providing a fifth relationship to B at bar 1: 6, and is again stated at bar 7: 9, with each of these moments acting as focal points in the overall texture. The closure of this opening number is accomplished by a shift from F♯, to which the word 'winter' is set, to a short descending bass motion from E to B, with D and C♯ constructing a linear connection between them. This passage provides a final reflection of the importance of these two pitches (E and B) and their ongoing juxtaposition, defining the harmonic basis and characterising the musical material of this initial chorus. This process is graphically summarised in Ex. 4.1.

2. The Argument

Alto Solo   Man has measured the heavens with a telescope, driven the gods
          from their thrones.
          But the soul, watching the chaotic mirror, knows that the gods
          return.
          Truly, the living god consumes within and turns the flesh to
          cancer!

Ex. 4.1 No. 1 (Chorus), principal pitch centres

This aria for alto solo, accompanied by obbligato wind, denies the conventions of the da capo aria, replacing its ABA shape with an image of progression. The writing for the wind instruments is in itself significant as it provides a dramatic contrast to that of the opening number; restricted in range, it provides a background to the soloist rather than engaging in a dialogue or commentary.

Following the previously stated B as the conclusion to the preceding number, E♭ is established as the pitch centre. Fifth-related pitches remain prominent, with the initial melodic gesture in the winds outlining a step-wise move from E♭ to B♭. The importance of these pitches is reinforced through the entry of the voice, which, in contrast to the step-wise motion of the previous wind parts, begins with a straightforward leap from E♭ to B♭. The use of pedal notes to give a sense of harmonic focus is again evident, with the shift from the prolonged F (bar 10: 1–) to B♭ (bar 10: 6) continuing to emphasise the fifth relationship. This move from F to B♭ also indicates Tippett's attempt to relate such points of structure to moments of significance within the text and its musical representation. The F (10: 1) provides the harmonic support for the word 'heavens', which is set to an alternation of E♭ and D♭, and the conclusion of the vocal phrase (G♭–F) coincides with the B♭ pedal.

However, the centrality of E♭ and its relationship to B♭ is subverted at bar 11: 6 through the introduction of B as the sustained bass. Conveying a sense of departure, this move coincides with the word 'thrones', which acts as a temporary conclusion to the vocal line and leads into a short instrumental passage (11: 8 – 12: 3). The focus on B leads to G (12: 4), which then rises to C (13: 1) before falling back to G. This motion to G at bar 13: 3 coincides with the fall from C to B in the melodic line, resolving on an implied G major harmony. This sense of resolution is reinforced and given dramatic effect by the ensuing silence of the next bar. The convergence between moments of structural and dramatic significance is again evident at figure 14, with the climactic word 'truly' (marked *ff*) supported by the return of E♭ in the strings. The juxtaposition of E♭ and

B♭ returns as a means of ending the number, with the E♭ at bar 16: 4 eventually leading to B♭ as the final event (figure 17).

Interludium (orchestra)

In contrast to the break that preceded it, the alto solo is followed by a brief interlude providing a greater degree of continuity between the second and third numbers. This continuity is established through the use of B♭ as a sustained pedal. The use of the flutes to carry the melodic interest is notable, as these were the only wind instruments not to be involved in the accompaniment to the previous alto solo; however, as in the previous number, the range is still restricted. This does not suggest that it is necessarily inexpressive. The tranquil, static nature of the texture (Meno mosso, tranquillo) contrasts with both the intensity of the previous alto solo and the drama of the following chorus. The importance of the minor third is tentatively indicated through the starting points for the contrapuntal texture between the two flutes, with the first beginning on A♭ and the second entering with an F which coincides with the repeated A♭ in the first flute. The fifth is also emphasised with the flute lines coming to a close on a vertical realisation of E♭ and B♭ (figure 19).

3. Scena

Chorus: Is evil then good?
　　　　Is reason untrue?
Alto: Reason is true to itself;
　　　　But pity breaks open the heart.
Chorus: We are lost.
　　　　We are as seed before the wind.
　　　　We are carried to a great slaughter.

Although the key signature now changes to one sharp, the initial vertical harmony clearly indicates a return to the pitch B. The B minor sonority in the first bar is articulated by the trombones, a textural recollection of the initial E minor sonority of the work. This retrospective glance is reinforced by a reference to the recently heard Interludium texture (bar 21: 7), which now sounds somewhat discontinuous with its immediate surroundings: an instance of Tippett's liking for differentiated textures. In between these two points the focus moves to D at bar 19: 12. Here the choral texture settles on a D major harmony, with this pitch sustained as the bass before moving through C♯ to B, a gesture which concludes the choral statement and recalls the trombones' initial B harmony. At bar 20: 1 the alto solo introduces a contrasting texture. Again D is central, with the voice beginning with a sustained statement of this pitch supported by the bass. However, the descending motion which follows introduces B♭ as a significant factor and avoids C♯, thus complicating the status of D. It moves eventually to a clarification of G at bar 21: 2, with G stated as the bass of the texture supporting B♭ and D in the strings while the first violin part rises from E through F♯ to G, a gesture which recollects the initial number (0: 5 – 0: 6). The return of the Interludium material at bar 21: 7, as suggested, contrasts with its previous appearance. Now A, rather than B♭, is the sustained bass line and the minor third formed between the starting pitches of the two flutes consists of G and E.

As well as the Interludium, the initial choral material of the number is also recalled (bar 24: 3) but in an expanded form and with a different pitch orientation. At the first instance the initial pitches are C/B imitated by F♯/F, but the return features a rising figure with D♯/E imitated by G♯/A (Exx. 4.2a and 4.2b). Although the pitch content is now transformed, the imitation ensures some similarity between the two moments. This passage, as well as the restatement of the Interludium material, provides an early illustration of Tippett's use of varied repetition: a process which, in preference to either more literal repetition or fully-fledged development, becomes a recurring characteristic of his musical language.

Figure 25 features the introduction of a short string-based texture which is discontinuous in relation to its surounding contexts but leads towards the return of the chorus at bars 25: 7/8. This new idea is built around the minor third formed between A♯ and C♯. The initial gesture consists of a rising motion from A♯ through B to C♯, while the final event restates B moving to C♯. This C♯ is taken up by the chorus, with the sopranos beginning with C♯ rising through D♯ to F♯. This choral texture is again imitative, with the C♯–D♯–F♯ figure eventually answered by B–C♯–E in the tenor part (26: 1); it remains consistent to the end of the

Ex. 4.2

(a)

(b)

number, providing the momentum by which Tippett gives musical substance to the impetus of the text ('We are as seed before the wind').

The final pitch of the number is E, which is sounded throughout the orchestra and is preceded by B as a cadential gesture. This final reference to E–B retrospectively sheds light on the initial B sonority: we can now hear it as a 'dominant' to E, emphasising both the fifth relationship in general and these pitches in particular.

4. The Narrator

> Bass solo Now in each nation there were some cast out by
>   authority and tormented,
>   made to suffer for the general wrong.
>   Pogroms in the east, lynching in the west;
>   Europe brooding on a war of starvation.
>   And a great cry went up from the people.

As discussed in chapter 2, this passage is clearly an attempt to reconstitute the recitative of Baroque oratorio within Tippett's own stylistic context (see Ex. 2.1). The parlando effect of the vocal writing provides an immediate contrast to the often florid melismatic vocal parts in other numbers, as does the reduced accompaniment after the full orchestral texture which concluded the previous scena. This accompaniment deliberately imitates the textures of recitative, with the arpeggiated string chords echoing the keyboard and the sustained bass line of the cello part providing a sense of harmonic focus. The first vertical harmony outlines an A major sonority which is followed by a sustained C# pedal. This C#/A context implies a dominant relationship to D, one which is never actually clarified within this passage. This shift away from the sequence of clearly defined harmonic centres in the previous numbers thus adds to the immediate sense of contrast, and the resulting ambiguity is reinforced through the continued avoidance of D in the following number.

The second and third appearances of the chordal texture contribute to the absence of any coherent harmonic focus, with bar 31: 1 consisting of the arpeggiation of an F# minor harmony and bar 32: 1 featuring F and A. However, the fact that A is sustained from this point and eventually rises to E (bar 32: 5) again suggests A as a centre; but now with the repeated C in the violin part it is A minor rather than A major which is implied. In fact, the final event consists of this repeated C, and the same pitch provides a point of continuity into the next movement (see Ex. 2. 2b). As indicated in chapter 2, this is Tippett's attempt to maintain a connection across the point of harmonic and textural change. However, this common-tone link is not sufficiently integrated to be interpreted as a unifying device: rather it is best understood as a point of anticipation through which the music moves into the following differentiated chorus.

5. The Chorus of the Oppressed

When shall the usurers' city cease,
And famine depart from the fruitful land?

The imitative nature of this chorus with its allusion to an already historicised musical gesture, has already been referred to in chapter 2 (see Ex. 2.2a). The change of key signature indicates F minor as the new harmonic centre. This tonality is also alluded to through the descending melodic gesture formed by the continued C which eventually falls to A♭.

This soprano line is imitated by the alto part, which begins on F and moves to D♭ (bars 33: 2 – 33: 5/6). The fifth relationship formed between F and C alludes to inherited traditions, with the point of imitation effectively corresponding to conventional expectations. The strict fugal nature of this chorus continues through the introduction of the tenor part on C (33: 6) and the bass on F (figure 34). The linear/contrapuntal texture continues to bar 36: 9; at which point the first distinctly vertical event occurs, with each line converging on a sustained D major harmony, a sonority which not only significantly shifts away from the initially implied F minor but also introduces a minor third relationship with F. The process of linear convergence towards this point of harmonic clarification, with each of the vocal parts in stepwise gravitation, results in a new-found coherence:

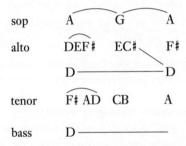

This moment of vertical harmony is immediately followed by the return of the imitative choral texture (bar 37: 2), with an initial exchange between A (alto) and D (tenor) which continues to support the emphasis on D.

The next change of harmonic centre begins with the change of key signature at bar 39: 3, which sees the music moving towards E. However, this motion is not direct, beginning from D (bar 39: 3); it is only at bar 39: 9 that E is first indicated and only at bar 40: 5 that this indication is realised through the rising bass motion of D–D♯–E. This process is confirmed at bar 41: 1 with the music settling on an E major chord as the concluding event of the number, a point of repose which provides a parallel to that at bar 36: 9 and thus creates a binary shape; but the references to D and E at these points now put a different perspective on the initial implied F minor harmony.

6. Tenor Solo

I have no money for my bread; I have no gift for my love.
I am caught between my desires and their frustration as
between the hammer and the anvil.
How can I grow to a man's stature?

This tenor solo is framed by a short string-based prelude and post-lude, with the prelude anticipating the main substance of the number. Tippett acknowledges his debt to Purcell for this formal device, as well as for the repetition of a short phrase when the voice does enter: 'Purcellian is the setting of the scene by a short orchestral introduction, and the manner of repeating a simple, easily understood phrase. Such a phrase is that to the first words the tenor solo sings – "I have no money for my bread".' This statement forms part of a longer essay on Purcell which indicates that his music provided an important source for specific moments in *A Child of Our Time*:

> I like to think I was influenced by Purcellian examples when I needed to express an aria from some of the relatively simple situations of *A Child of Our Time*.
>   I am thinking particularly of the air for tenor to a tango-like bass – an air which had to express the frustrations of the ordinary man temporarily at odds with life. The things that influence one, in a composition of this kind, are never simple, but always complex. The sense of our time – that is, in this case, of the period between the world wars – lies musically in the tango, not in any Purcellian turn of phrase.[1]

This reference to the tango reflects Tippett's concern with the contemporary nature of his subject matter. The use of the popular idiom to invoke the 'ordinary' provides a parallel to the use of the spiritual as a more generalised symbol.

The clarification of E at the conclusion of the previous chorus provides continuity here, with this pitch now functioning as a sustained pedal note to the initial texture of the accompaniment. Above this pedal note the violin line outlines yet another rising minor third formed through E, F♯ and G. The pitch centre changes from E to C at bar 42: 5, with C now functioning as the sustained pedal note. This leads to a change of key signature and the now repeated C indicating C minor. The entry of the tenor solo above this texture at bar 43: 4, which Tippett himself describes as 'a tango-like bass', again highlights the minor third: C is the initial and final pitch and E♭ appears as the high-point of the opening melodic line. Of more general significance is the glance towards the popular idiom as defined by the 'tango-like bass', which adds yet another differentiated stylistic reference and exemplifies Tippett's allusive practice.[2] E returns as the harmonic centre at bar 46: 4. This point of return is given added significance as it provides support for what is a crucial dramatic moment in the text, with the words 'How can I grow to a man's stature' isolated in relation to what has come before, and the immediately preceding cadential effect also reinforces its dramatic and musical significance. Further reinforcement comes through the deployment of the E–F♯–G gesture in the first violin part, in a partially concealed recollection.

There is a move to B at bar 47: 6 which coincides with the return of the initial instrumental texture, but now the initial E–F♯–G gesture is transposed to B–C♯–D. The shift between these two pitches (E and B) once again exemplifies the significance of their specific relationship and of the fifth relationship in general. However, it is G that is established as the final pitch centre of the number at figure 49. This shift to G can be seen retrospectively in relation to the initial E as a continuing emphasis on the minor third, in the context both of this number and of what has preceded it.

7. Soprano Solo

> How can I cherish my man in such days, or become a
> mother in a world of destruction?
> How shall I feed my children on so small a wage?
> How can I comfort them when I am dead?

In contrast to the previous number, this aria is open-ended, with a sense of forward momentum avoiding any suggestion of formal repetition. The number begins with an extensive instrumental introduction which anticipates the main melodic characteristics of the aria and, in terms of its static and transparent texture, provides a marked contrast to the 'tango' identity of the previous number. The key signature of G minor, introduced in the final bars of the previous number, indicates that G will continue to function as the pitch centre. However, the initial linear

Ex. 4.3

chromatic writing complicates this notion and it is not until bar 50: 2 that G minor is realised as a vertical harmony. The vertical texture at bars 50 – 50: 3 provides a moment of focus and clarity in relation to the essentially linear texture and the return of this vertical idea at bars 50: 6 and 52: 2 helps lend a sense of shape to the initial moments of the accompaniment. These points of vertical focus also involve a highly distinctive interaction with the linear dimension, with each point coinciding with a descending melodic gesture. The semitone inflexion has already been anticipated through the somewhat fragmentary introduction and is continued into the melismatic writing for the soprano solo. The voice enters at bar 50: 6 in convergence with the vertical harmony based on B♭ (Ex. 4.3). The sustained F falls to E♮, which provides a reflection of the initial exchange between C♯ and B♯ and again the G/F♯ at figure 50. The vocal phrase concludes at figure 52 with the descent from B♭ to A confirming the local significance of the semitone inflexion.

From here on this extended melodic gesture in the voice is repeated and expanded, giving a sense of enlargement and growth throughout the number. The convergence between the vertical harmony and the melodic gesture (bars 50: 6 and 52: 2) also interacts with a significant point in the text, with both moments providing a realisation of 'How' as the starting point of the soprano soloist's dramatic questioning of the situation. The third (bar 53: 9) and fourth (bar 54: 9) statements of this word also share a textural idea, but now it is the semitone which is picked up from the introduction and stated against a wind-based texture also featuring the initial semitone. The fifth representation of 'How' is based on the return of the initial interaction of the vertical harmony and the main melodic gesture (bar 55: 7). Now it is A♭, as part of an F minor harmony, which provides the musical focus on this conspicuous textural detail. The sixth and final presentation (bar 56: 5) provides a direct parallel to bar 55: 7 with the melodic G♭ forming part of an E♭ minor harmony.

The final moments of this number contain what is perhaps the most musically effective moment in the work, effecting a sense of association with the spiritual that will conclude Part I. Following the poetically climactic setting of 'when I am dead', which is given added significance through its silent background, the semitone figure is repeated as C–B♮–C at bar 58: 8 and is extended to rise to E♭, with the C and E♭ combining to form a statement of the minor third element. From figure 59 the semitone is repeated, moving from C/B to D/E♭ with the melodic line finally reaching to G, which is then sustained and held over into the following spiritual, at which point it forms the new tonic. (This common-tone link between two separate numbers has already been used between Nos. 4 and 5.) As at that point the effect is not that of unification, the repetition of G creates a greater sense of anticipation than of unification; but now the effect is that of focusing attention, through the now slow-moving accompaniment and gradually rising melody, towards the impending harmonic stasis of the spiritual.

8. A Spiritual

Chorus and Soli Steal away, steal away, steal away to Jesus;
Steal away, steal away home –

I han't got long to stay here.

My lord, He calls me, He calls me by the thunder,
The trumpet sounds within-a my soul,
I han't got long to stay here.

Green trees a-bending, poor sinner stand a-trembling,
The trumpet sounds within-a my soul,
I han't got long to stay here.

Steal away, steal away, steal away to Jesus;
Steal away, Steal away home –
I han't got long to stay here.

Although this link between the soprano solo and the spiritual is highly effective, the two numbers are in many ways sharply contrasted. The soprano solo was defined through the recurring semitone figure and a prevailing harmonic ambiguity, an ambiguity which largely resulted through the linear/contrapuntal texture. In contrast, the spiritual is explicitly diatonic and firmly rooted in its G major tonality. However, Tippett's attempt to forge a connection between the two numbers is again evident in some of the specific details. For example, the C/B and D/E♭ semitone figure of figure 59 and bar 59: 2 etc. could be seen as an anticipatory transformation of the D/E figure of bar 59: 10 in the spiritual, particularly as the rhythmic shape of the figure remains intact (see Ex. 4.4). But, as will become clear in the next chapter, such points of association do not necessarily imply any greater degree of integration and/or unity.

Part II

The second part of the overall tripartite shape is the most extended of the three, consisting of seventeen clearly defined, individually identified numbers, and, as a consequence, the most diffuse in terms of its harmonic and textural character. This more differentiated musical surface is also partly generated through the increase in specific numbers for the Narrator, all of which tend to be more ambiguous in terms of harmony/pitch centre and somewhat fragmentary in terms of texture, particularly in comparison to the surrounding contexts.

Ex. 4.4

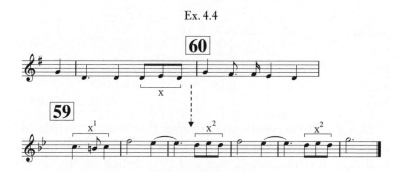

9. Chorus

A star rises in mid winter.
Behold the man! The scape-goat!
The child of our time.

This number begins with the introduction of the D major/B minor key signature and suggests a possible continuity through the retrospective formation of a fifth relationship between the implied D and the concluding G of the previous number. However, other than as a consequence of the introduction of the new key signature, it is difficult to hear either D or B as the new pitch centre as the opening bars are defined through the alteration of G and F♯, an ambiguity which suggests the continuing influence of G. The first indication of D comes in the third and fourth bars through the linear ascent from C♯ to D; however, the avoidance of any clearly defined vertical harmony reinforces the essential ambiguity of the texture.

The entry of the choral parts at figure 62 again draws attention towards Tippett's liking for imitative vocal textures and thus recalls the opening of the work. This imitation, in conjunction with the Largo tempo indication, has a somewhat static effect which reflects the contemplative nature of the subject matter. The semitone inflexion formed between C♯ and D in the third bar is now expanded as the starting point of the vocal entries, with these entries corresponding to the expectations of the fifth relationship (G–D/F♯–C♯):

```
            62
soprano         G ——— F♯
                D —— C♯
alto                G ——— F♯
tenor                       D —— C♯
bass                            G ——— F♯
```

At figure 63 the initial texture returns, thus creating a refrain-like process, but this return incorporates a slight variation in the pitch of the final element of the gesture, with G/F♯/G♯ replacing G/F♯/G. The resulting convergence of repetition and variation is continued at figure 64 as the imitative vocal parts return but lowered by a semitone, with D/C♯ and G/F♯ replaced by G♭/F and D♭/C. This texture now inevitably returns to the opening gesture but now it is F♯ moving to A which is utilised (bar 64: 4). This process of interacting patterns of repetition and slight variation, which suggests that Tippett is appropriating the conventions of sequential motion, can be summarised as follows:

```
                62              63
      G–F♯–G      G/F♯D/C♯      G–F♯–G♯


                64              64:4
            G♭/FD♭/C        F♯–A–F♯
```

The imitative vocal texture reappears at bar 65: 2 but now the focus changes from the semitone back to the minor third. This is clearly evident in the soprano and alto parts, which feature both linear and vertical realisations of this interval:

```
soprano    ⌐F  ⌐D   ⌐C   B
           |   |    |
alto       └D  └B   └A   G
```

From this point on there is a greater continuity and expansion. The resulting sense of momentum leads towards the statement of the words 'The child of our time' (66: 3 – 67: 2). The setting of these dramatically significant words is, as Kemp demonstrates, again built around the repe-

Ex. 4.5

Handel: Messiah, Part II

Tippett (65 : 2)

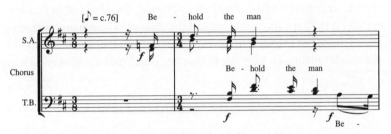

tition of the minor third, with the fall from A to F♯ in the soprano (bar 66: 4) being followed by the descent from E to C♯ in the alto part (figure 67).[3] If the identification of a stable pitch centre for the opening of the number was problematic, then, in contrast, the point of conclusion is relatively straightforward, with the final descending motion from C♯ through B to F♯ providing a point of repose after the momentum of the preceding material. This arrival on F♯ is also of importance in terms of larger pitch relationships. If, retrospectively, we can accept B rather than D as the implied initial pitch centre then we can see the fifth relationship formed between B and F♯ as once again significant.

Meirion Bowen suggests that this number is directly based on the chorus which opens Part II of *Messiah*, 'Behold the Lamb of God'.[4] The similarity is not restricted to the obvious parallel between Tippett's 'Behold the Man' and the text of the Handel extract. As Ex. 4.5 illustrates, the melodic gesture is similar, as is its rhythmic identity, with

Handel's octave leap transformed into Tippett's rising sixth, formed initially between F and D. This brief example provides some insight into Tippett's relationship to the Handel model in particular and indicates how the work's intertextual practice is not restricted to the literary dimension.

10. The Narrator

Bass Solo And a time came when in the continual persecution
one race stood for all.

This brief passage is entirely anticipatory in relation to the following chorus. As with the numbers for the Narrator in Part I, the texture is a reflection of Tippett's awareness of previous musical conventions, with the reference to recitative again being obvious. Also identical in relation to Part I is the harmonic ambiguity of the passage. The initial chord outlines B major but the vocal line involves passing references which contradict this B tonality, for example B♭ (bar 68: 3) and A♭ (bars 68: 4 and 5).

11. Double Chorus of Persecutors and Persecuted

Away with them!
Curse them! Kill them!
They infect the state.

Where? How? Why?
We have no refuge.

However, the initial B major effect of the previous narration is now given an implied function through the change of key signature to four sharps at the beginning of this chorus: the suggestion that it now functions retrospectively as dominant to the new key of E major is reinforced through the concluding gesture of the vocal line, with the ascent from C through C♯/ D to D♯ seeming to anticipate a realisation of E (bars 68: 8/9). Nevertheless, the specific musical details appear to complicate the simplicity of this interpretation. For example, the introductory imitative string texture of this number involves a degree of chromaticism which tends to obscure the implied tonality, with a move towards G♯ at figure 70 suggesting this pitch as 'dominant' to C♯ (an implication already formed at the conclusion of the previous number through the sustained G♯ in the cello part (bar 68: 9)).

The choral parts involve a direct dialogue between the two choruses (Persecutors and Persecuted). The texture of each chorus is simplified in order to clarify the dramatic relationship between the two groups, with the stark juxtaposition of bold but short melodic gestures intensifying the immediacy of the moment. This exchange leads to a radical change of texture at bar 71: 9 which involves a repeated slow-moving pedal effect on F♯, above which the voices articulate a straightforward vertical statement consisting exclusively of A. At bar 72: 5 F♯ falls to C♯ in the accompaniment and then the vocal parts move from A to G♯, a motion which effectively signifies the conclusion of the number and the confirmation of C♯ as the central harmonic reference for the number as a whole.

12. The Narrator

Bass Solo Where they could, they fled from the terror.
And among them a boy escaped secretly, and was kept
in hiding in a great city.

As is now clearly expected with the passages for the Narrator, this brief narration is harmonically ambiguous, having little sense of its own immediately identifiable pitch centre, and, like the previous narrative passages, it functions as a recitative in anticipation of the following chorus.

13. Chorus of the Self-righteous

We cannot have them in our Empire.
They shall not work, nor beg a dole.
Let them starve in No–Man's–Land!

This choral number remains harmonically ambiguous. The key signature seems to indicate a C-based tonality, an interpretation which is endorsed by Kemp's analysis.[5] However, in terms of the initial material, G seems to enjoy a certain degree of priority, since the first two bars are characterised through the rise from G to D in the cello part. The main melodic gesture of the number again features the minor third as a conspicuous element, with the initial exchange between the oboe and flute parts being built around this interval: B♭–G in the oboe and F–D in the flute. The choral entries in the third bar again draw attention to Tippett's liking for imitative textures, but now it is the fifth relationship, rather than the minor third, which provides the main characteristic of the gesture in the form of an initial rise from G to C (alto). This rise is echoed by a move from A to D (tenor) and then descents from G (soprano) and C (bass). At bar 74: 9 the minor third element (x) is given renewed focus through the transfer of the initial oboe/flute gesture into the choral parts but the connection with the fifth relationship (y) as defined through the process of imitation remains a significant factor (Ex. 4.6). The repetition which emerges as a consequence of the imitative process again produces a somewhat static texture and provides a degree of contrast to the dramatic immediacy of the previous Double Chorus (No. 11).

The conclusion of the vocal entries at bar 75: 3 leads into a return of the initial bass theme, now doubled in the cello and double bass parts. This moment provides a further reflection of the increasing significance of such points of return and repetition within discrete sections of the work. The number concludes with a point of arrival on B, with the words 'in No-Man's-Land', which – following the moments of focus on G – seems to call into question Kemp's identification of C as the pitch centre. Nevertheless, it is perhaps possible to interpret the apparent centrality of G as forming part of a 'dominant' (= fifth relationship) to an implied but seemingly absent C.

14. The Narrator

Bass Solo And the boy's mother wrote a letter, saying:

This next insertion for the Narrator once again does not achieve its own immediate identity but rather serves as a prelude to the following extended scena. The relationship to what comes next is based on the F♯ which functions as the bass of the initial vertical harmony of the quasi-recitative texture and which will eventually provide a 'leading note' link to the central G in the scena. This sense of anticipation is a direct reflection of the text, in which the Narrator's introduction of the image of the Mother writing a letter paves the way for the dramatically and musically expansive scena.

Ex. 4.6

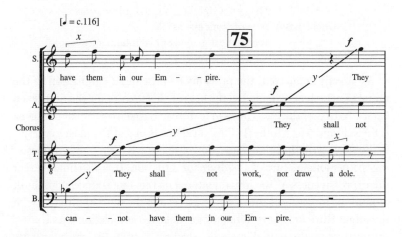

15. *Scena*

Solo Quartet
Mother (Soprano): O my Son! In the dread terror they
have brought me near to death.
Boy (Tenor): Mother! Mother!
Though men hunt me like an animal, I will
defy the world to reach you.

Aunt (Alto): Have patience.
Throw not your life away in futile sacrifice.
Uncle (Bass): You are as one against all.
Accept the impotence of your humanity.
Boy: No! I must save her.

As already suggested, the previous F♯ provides a connection to the initial G, which is sustained as the bass of this texture for the first seven bars. The first of the four voices to feature in the solo quartet of the scena is the soprano (the Mother). This vocal line is one of the most evocative in the work, with the initial repetition of the words 'O my son' emphasising the personal nature of the dramatic situation. It is also notable that the expressiveness of the initial material of this line is once again built around the intervals of the minor third (x) and the fourth/fifth (y), with the minor third being exploited for its inherited associations. As Ex. 4.7 demonstrates, the initial melodic gesture consists of the step-wise descent from D to C followed by the rising minor third formed between C and E♭. This gesture is then immediately repeated, but is transposed to begin on E♭ and then rise from D to F, again providing a small-scale illustration of the increasing use of seemingly fragmentary sequential gestures. The importance of the fifth relationship emerges between the fifth and sixth bars, with what is effectively the second phrase beginning with a conspicuous leap from C to G on the word 'dread'. It is also notable that this G forms the registral high point of the soprano line and is framed by D as the initial pitch and A as the point of ending on the word 'death'. Thus the line can be seen to be framed by the fifth relationship:

bar   77   77:5   77:8
           D ——————————— G ——————————— A

The sense of potential closure on A is reinforced by the melodic descent from B♭ to A, with the falling semitone providing an image of resolution. This melodic arrival on A coincides with a shift from G through C finally to D in the bass, which is then sustained for four bars. The move from G to D clearly imitates a 'tonic' to 'dominant' progression, but it also parallels the D–G element in the melodic line outlined above.

This focus on D leads into an abrupt change of texture at bar 78: 2 and the introduction of the tenor solo (the Boy). The brass replace the strings as the accompaniment, and the vocal writing is now more declamatory

Ex. 4.7

and disjunct in contrast to the expressive lyricism of the soprano line. Again the minor third and fifth relationships are significant factors in the vocal line, with the opening gesture consisting of a rising minor third formed between G and B♭ (bar 78: 2) and the line effectively closing with a gesture which consists of a rise from C♯ to F♯ followed by a step-wise descent back to the C♯ (78: 6).

This arrival on C♯ is then immediately followed by another somewhat abrupt change of texture (78: 7) which again forms a more static accompaniment, now in the form of an initial alternation between D♭ and D♮ in the violin parts and a linear descent in the cello part which extends from the initial F to the arrival on E♭ at bar 79: 2. The accompaniment supports the introduction of the alto solo (the Aunt), with the repetitions mirroring the words 'Have patience'; it continues into the introduction of the bass solo (the Uncle) at figure 79. This brief overlap contrasts with the previously disjunct vocal entries and accompanying textures. Following the reappearance of the tenor solo, the number ends with a sequence of vertical harmonies which concludes on a stable G major sonority.

16. A Spiritual

Chorus and Soli Nobody knows the trouble I see, Lord,
                    Nobody knows like Jesus.

                    O brothers, pray for me,
                    O brothers, pray for me,
                    And help me to drive
                    Old satan away.

> O mothers, pray for me,
> O mothers, pray for me,
> And help me to drive
> Old satan away.
>
> Nobody knows the trouble I see, lord,
> Nobody knows like Jesus.

As already suggested, this spiritual can be interpreted as the effective centre of the work. Its explicit C minor tonality, however, distances it from its immediate surrounding contexts and the only real preparation for it comes in the form of the final G sonority to the previous number, suggesting a 'dominant-to-tonic' relationship between the two numbers. It has already been noted in the introduction to this chapter, that the minor third formed between G and B♭ in the second bar of the melody, along with the fifth formed between the initial C and G, has the potential to be interpreted as providing a source for the recurrences of these intervals throughout the work, but, as will be clarified in the next chapter, this suggestion is in itself loaded with contentious assumptions.

17. Scena

Duet – Bass and Alto Soli
Narrator: The boy becomes desperate in his agony.
Alto: A curse is born.
The dark forces threaten him.
Narrator: He goes to authority.
He is met with hostility.
Alto: His other self rises in him, demonic and destructive.
Narrator: He shoots the official –
Alto: But he shoots only his dark brother –
And see – he is dead.

This duet begins with a recollection of the Narrator's texture, with the bass solo being introduced by a recitative-like spread chord outlining the first inversion of a B minor harmony. Like previous insertions for the Narrator, this passage gives a commentary on the next stage of the drama, indicating the desperation of the boy's situation. The stability of the initial B harmony is immediately questioned by the vocal line, which includes inflexions on A♭ and B♭. The resulting disruption is also evident in the accompaniment, which moves quickly towards the alternation of B♭ and F in the fourth bar. The arrival on B♭ at this point is reinforced through its assumption of a cadential role. It is also repeated throughout bars 82: 8 to 82: 10 and provides a harmonic support to the introduction of the alto solo.

The writing for the alto is contrasted to that for the bass, the former providing a degree of lyricism in contrast to the somewhat angular nature of the latter. However, although this contrast between the two voices continues throughout the number and is clearly its defining factor, within the accompaniment a distinct sense of harmonic motion – predicated on the fifth relationship, a process which originates from the B♭/F element outlined above – emerges. Following the apparent stability of B♭, the eighth and ninth bars feature a move from A to E, with E then assuming some semblance of stability. This leads to the sustained G at bar 83: 3, which again fulfils a fifth relationship through its association with C at bar 83: 5. After this point of arrival on C, there is again a moment of seeming stability, but this is somewhat transient as C quickly moves to C♯ and then B before F♯ appears at bar 83: 9. The arrival on F♯ coincides with the bass soloist's presentation of the words 'He shoots the official'. This almost matter-of-fact presentation of this symbolic act within the drama is a memorable moment of understatement, a gesture which by its very simplicity attracts attention to itself. In terms of pitch content the melodic gesture consists of a descent from B (83: 8) to G♯ (83: 9), but with chromatic motions through A♯ and A filling in the minor-third space.

The inflexions on B and C♯ in the bass line can now be seen as further manifestations of the fifth relationship in connection to this F♯ (83: 9), but the focus on F♯ also forms an association with the final moment of the number, which consists of an arrival on C♯. The entire process can be summarised in the following way:

bars 82: 7/8	82: 11/12	83: 3 – 83: 5	83: 7 – 83: 9
B♭–F	A–E	G–C	C♯–B–F♯

83: 9 – 84: 3
F♯–C♯

The final focus on C♯ consists of a descending minor third from E to C♯, with the alto stating the words 'And see he is dead' to these pitches along with D♯. Once again, this moment presents an interface between structural and dramatic factors. The minor third not only returns as a recurring intervallic characteristic; it is also associated with the word 'dead'.

18. The Narrator

Bass solo They took a terrible vengeance.

By this stage we have certain expectations concerning the passages for the Narrator, and this number corresponds exactly to these expectations. The initial vertical texture implies an A-based harmony but the passage is too brief to enable any sense of harmonic or textural identity to emerge. Following the brief vocal statement there is a four-bar orchestral gesture which is entirely preparatory to what comes next, anticipating certain main features of the following chorus such as the minor third formed between C♯ and E (bars 84: 8 – 84: 10).

19. The Terror

Chorus Burn down their houses! Beat in their heads!
Break them in pieces on the wheel!

This extensive and elaborate choral number again highlights Tippett's liking for imitative textures and inherited conventions, with fugue providing a formal archetype. However, although the chorus is defined through its fugal identity, the actual thematic content continues to reflect the main recurring intervallic features of the work: the minor third and fifth relationships. This is made evident in Ex. 4.8, which identifies the conspicuous use of these intervals within the fugue subject as it initially appears in the tenor part throughout the first six bars. The minor third (*x*) formed between C♯ and E has already been anticipated in the previous number but now it clearly forms part of the melodic identity of the subject. Also notable is the fact that the first melodic gesture begins with C and ends on A, providing a more extended reflection of the minor third. The second unit of the subject is again built around the minor third, with the rise from E to G in the third and fourth bars providing a certain parallel to the C♯/E interval in the first bar. The third and final unit, beginning with the A♯ in bar 85: 5, does not continue with this

Ex. 4.8

melodic idea, but it is notable that it concludes with a rise of a fifth: from G to D (*y*). This concluding gesture then continues to be realised, as expected, through the sequence of fugal entries:

bar 85: 2	85: 8	86: 4	87
		(soprano) C	
	(alto) G		
(tenor) C			
			(bass) G

Following these entries, the continuation of this number is conditioned through the working out of the fugal process. Although Tippett does not always fully combine the historical archetype with his own evolving musical language, in this instance he is able to bring the fugal process into the context of the work as a whole through the exploitation of the fifth relationship: the common element between both the fugal archetype and that which surrounds it within this immediate context.

20. The Narrator

Bass solo Men were ashamed of what was done.
There was bitterness and horror.

This passage begins with a sustained C minor harmony. However, as with the previous numbers for the Narrator, this does not signify a period of harmonic stability. Following the initial statement of C, the bass line falls to B at bar 90: 7 and then to A before moving to B♭ at bar 91: 2. This B♭ then moves through C to D♭ on which the number concludes. It is difficult to interpret the significance of this 'progression', as it does not seem to imply any direct sense of preparation for the harmonic stability of the subsequent spiritual. However, as F minor will form the tonality of the spiritual, we can hear the initial C minor as forming a fifth relationship to that tonality. Although these questions concerning the harmonic identity of the passage are pertinent, the main function of the passage is in setting the scene for what comes next, just as the text reflects on the consequences of the previous actions as a preparation for the dramatic position of the subsequent spiritual.

21. A Spiritual of Anger

Chorus and Bass Solo　Go down Moses, 'way down in Egypt land;
Tell old Pharaoh, to let my people go.

When Israel was in Egypt's land,
Let my people go,
Oppressed so hard they could not stand,
Let my people go,
'Thus spake the Lord', bold Moses said,
Let my people go,
'If not, I'll smite your first-born dead',
Let my people go.

Go down, Moses, 'way down in Egypt land;
Tell old Pharaoh, to let my people go.

Kemp describes the 'spiritual of anger' as 'set as a chorale prelude, the tune a cantus firmus while canonic counterpoints deriving from it weave above'.[6] This is an accurate description of the texture. The choral realisation of the spiritual text is simple and direct, while the orchestral accompaniment is a complex flowing contrapuntal texture which provides an effective background to the text. Kemp's idea of the 'chorale prelude' is also of interest, as it again raises the question of Tippett's use of inherited models. The importance of the Bach Passions has already been indicated, and while drawing on the chorale prelude need not imply another direct debt to that specific musical context, it is, at the very least, a glance towards J. S. Bach.

The harmonic simplicity of this spiritual contrasts with what has come before, with its F minor tonality and its dependency on basic diatonic harmonies made explicit from the outset; as an obvious consequence of its tonality, the minor third is again deployed as a melodic interval, the most clear instance being the repetition of A♭–F (92: 1 etc.).

22. The Boy Sings in his Prison

Tenor Solo My dreams are all shattered in a ghastly reality.
The wild beating of my heart is stilled: day by day.
Earth and sky are not for those in prison.
Mother! Mother !

This number begins with an extended duet between violins and flutes which is once again based on imitation, with the flutes introducing a condensed version of the violin theme. The imitative texture provides what Kemp describes as a 'period of reflection'[7] and it certainly provides a brief suspension in the momentum of the dramatic narrative. It is also interesting from the intervallic perspective. The minor third is again prominent, providing a frame to the theme (which begins on G and concludes on E). The entry of the tenor solo also uses the minor third to frame a melodic statement, with the initial C falling to A in bar 95: 3. This minor third is immediately echoed by the descent from B to G♯. Both statements of the interval portray the word 'shattered', with the repetition providing a poignant intensity as well as again highlighting the expressive significance of this structurally important interval. The second vocal phrase outlines another main recurring interval, the fifth, with B (bar 95: 4) moving to E (bar 95: 7). This initial vocal line is underpinned by the harmonic stability of the sustained A which eventually descends to E at bar 95: 7 and thus coincides with the arrival of the vocal line on E. The harmonic motion provides another fifth relationship, but E is also significant in its own right as it signifies a moment of harmonic and melodic arrival which also provides a focus on the text's 'ghastly reality'.

The next entry of the tenor solo (bar 95: 8) begins on F and ascends to Ab (figure 96). However, as the line first descends, diverging from the previous material, this minor third is not so clearly identifiable. The new idea takes the form of an increase in the melodic motion which is clearly intended to reflect 'The wild beating of my heart', together with a decrease in motion to the repetition of 'stilled'. Such a response to the text demonstrates Tippett's awareness of the dramatic potential of 'word-painting', a potential he first realised through his involvement with the music of Purcell.

The vocal line, and its harmonic support, converges towards Eb (bar 97: 3). This arrival on Eb parallels the arrival on E at bar 95: 7, but it also leads into a return of the initial violin and flute texture, which is now also presented at a new pitch level. The violin line begins on Bb as opposed to G, and the flute line moves from this Bb to G (figure 98). The formal return of this material can be seen as a ritornello, providing another reflection of Tippett's use of historicised models. The melodic arrival on G leads into the return of the tenor solo and its repetition of 'Mother' (bar 98: 1). This vocal statement is supported by the repetition of C in the lower strings which, after four bars, moves to A. This move reinforces the significance of the minor third within this number, but it also glances retrospectively towards the initial stability of A at figure 95.

23. The Mother

Soprano Solo What have I done to you, my son?
What will become of us now?
The springs of hope are dried up.
My heart aches in unending pain.

This number is imbued with many of what are by now the recurring characteristics of the work: pedal notes, implied tonal centres, the minor third. It begins with a sequence of repeated Ds in the bass part, implying this pitch as a centre. However, the repeated D ascends to B and then F# (bar 99: 4), forming an extended arpeggiation of B minor and now suggesting this as the possible tonality of the number. Above this extended arpeggiation a sequence of imitative melodic fragments appear, all of which invoke the minor third:

bar 98: 7   :8   99   99: 1   :2   :3
(Ob.) F–D (Fl.) D–F   (Vlc.) C–A   (Fl.) A–C   (Ob.) F–D   (Fl.) D–F
                                                                                (Vl.) A–F♯

These shapes are projected against the consistency of the bass line, reflecting the anxiety of the dramatic situation as the Mother comes to contemplate, 'What have I done . . .?' They are also featured in the writing for the soprano solo. The voice enters at figure 100, above the return of the repeated D pedal, with a melodic gesture which begins with a rise from D to F. From this point a certain lyrical expansion occurs. The melodic line moves towards the arrival on B at bar 101: 4. The focus on B at this point is significant as this pitch now provides a moment of melodic closure in relation to the initial D and the reintroduction of the pedal effect, now on B, also refers back to D, producing an extended, linear manifestation of the minor third but also reflecting the initial harmonic ambiguity between these two pitches which was indicated at the outset.

The extended lyricism of the solo part continues to define the number through to its conclusion. The sense of conclusion is generated through the arrival on F♯ as a moment of harmonic stasis between bars 103: 4 and the end of the number. This newly established F♯ now connects with B (bar 101: 4) and the initial D to provide both an extended realisation of the B minor arpeggio first outlined within the opening bars and a linear background to the number as a whole.

24. Alto Solo

The dark forces rise like a flood.
Men's hearts are heavy: they cry for peace.

This brief number for the alto solo functions as a prelude to the following spiritual. Once again the vocal writing is characterised by the use of the minor third, with the initial gesture consisting of an arpeggiation of E♭ minor followed by E minor (bars 103: 17/18). The final moment of the vocal line, on the word 'peace', is also formed by the minor third, A♯–C♯ (bar 104: 1). This statement coincides with the repetition of C♯–E in the violins, which forms a connection to what follows.

It is possible to see this transitional alto solo as somewhat flawed in relation to its surrounding contexts, as its slow-moving texture (Grave) detracts from the impact of the following spiritual. This view is supported by Kemp, who states that 'the transitional alto solo reverts to a slow tempo again and as a result the effect of the exquisitely beautiful setting of the spiritual is somewhat vitiated'.[8] It is clearly difficult to hear this moment as an effective transition to the spiritual, particularly in comparison to the effectiveness of the moment of anticipation from the soprano solo (No. 7) to the setting of 'Steal away' which concluded Part I, and it again anticipates the later discussion concerning problems of integration of the spirituals into the musical environment which Tippett constructed around them.

25. A Spiritual

Chorus and Soprano Solo O, by and by, by and by,
I'm going to lay down my heavy load.

I know my robe's going to fit me well,
I tried it on at the gates of hell.

O, hell is deep and a dark despair,
O, stop, poor sinner, and don't go there!

O, by and by, by and by,
I'm going to lay down my heavy load.

Like the previous spirituals, this number presents a moment of harmonic certainty and focus in relation to its surrounding context. The increasing focus on the minor third as a melodic element up to this point provides a certain connection to this spiritual, whose A major tonality also presents the interval, particularly in the form of F♯–A.

Part III

In contrast to the often somewhat harmonically diffuse and texturally contrasted nature of Part II, this final stage of the tripartite design has a more overt sense of harmonic direction and focus. This new-found cohesion is partly explained by the absence of the Narrator (the passages of narration often being the most harmonically and texturally diffuse of the work) and by the fact that, again in contrast to Part II, Part III consists of only five distinct numbers, as well as a Preludium to No. 29, all of which have their own sense of self-contained identity and are more extensive than certain earlier stages of the work.

26. Chorus

The cold deepens.
The world descends into the icy waters where lies the jewel of great price.

The slow-moving texture of this chorus recalls the initial numbers of both Parts I and II. The number begins with a short string-based introduction which establishes C♯ as the bass of the harmony. However, this quickly rises to F♯ to provide a quasi-cadential gesture which is consistent with the introduction of the F♯ minor key signature. The confirmation of F♯ minor establishes some continuity with the A major spiritual which concluded Part II, within which, as already indicated, F♯–A was a recognisable melodic feature. The chorus enters in the third bar with a chordal texture which begins on F♯ but descends to the vertical realisation of the fifth relationship formed between G and D (figure 107), a motion which anticipates the text's image of descent as stated by the words 'The cold deepens' (Ex. 4.9c). This chordal texture returns at bar 107: 3 but now it moves from B to C/G, again portraying the image of descent with the repetition of the initial lines of the text. This repetition/variation is somewhat reminiscent of those in the initial choruses of Parts I (bars 3: 7/9) and II (62: 3), in which points of vertical texture in the choral parts coincide with key moments in the text (Ex. 4.9a, b, c). Between the two choral entries (106: 10 and 107: 3), the initial string texture returns, but now moving from A in the upper part and F♯ in the bass towards the realisation of the fifth relationship between B and F♯ (107: 3), with B providing a point of connection between this string texture and the choral parts. The closure of the choral statement on C/G (figure 108) is now contrasted by a wind-based texture, introducing some discontinuity with the previous repetition in the string and choral parts.

The next choral entry (bar 108: 4) consists of the words 'The world descends', which are set to a descending line in the soprano part, falling from D♭ to F♯. This F♯ is supported by D in the bass, which has been preceded by C♯, giving an impression of a D major tonality. The second

Ex. 4.9

(a)

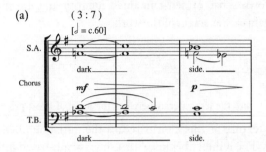

(b)

(c)

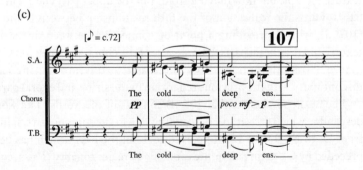

part of this melodic gesture again descends, but now to C/E♭ with A♭ also present in the tenor part (109: 2). At this point (109: 3) a new linear texture is introduced, a return to the extended imitation evident at many earlier stages in the score. The initial element of the line consists of D–D–E♭ (soprano). This is imitated by the altos with G–G–F♯, and the tenors and basses repeat this exchange. Again we see Tippett using the conventional expectations of the imitative process, but the prominence given to the fifth as a consequence produces a degree of consistency with other melodic and textural ideas. It is also notable that this linear passage arrives on the vertical realisation of an E major sonority (110: 1): a seemingly conventional gesture, but one which is some distance from the initial F♯ minor tonality and is not defined by a surrounding harmonic context. This clarification of E leads into a return of the wind-based texture, which now involves a recollection of the choral material from bar 109: 3. Now it is A that initiates the imitative texture and forms a fifth relationship with the vertical realisation of E (110: 1).

Figure 111 features a return of the texture first heard at figure 109 but now beginning on B♭ and gravitating towards G/D (111: 2) and F/A♭ (111: 3). The unaccompanied imitation returns at 111: 4 but now beginning on G/C and moving towards an A major sonority (112: 2). The changes involved in these points of return demonstrate again how Tippett is increasingly concerned with the interaction between repetition and variation. The number concludes with a bass motion from G♯ to C♯, providing both a final cadential gesture and a parallel to the move from C♯ to F♯ with which the number began. But perhaps it is the larger association formed between the initial F♯ tonality and the final move to C♯ which is of greater significance as this fifth relationship now provides a framework for the number as a whole, a process which has also been evident at earlier stages in the score.

In retrospect this number can be seen to be conditioned by the juxtaposition of two basic musical archetypes which have their origin in the text: the image of descent as represented by the descending vertical choral harmonies (107, 108, 109, 111) and what in retrospect can be heard as the expansive lyricism of the imitative realisation of 'where lies the jewel of great price' (110, 112).

27. Alto Solo

The soul of man is impassioned like a woman.
She is old as the earth, beyond good and evil,
the sensual garments.
Her face will be illuminated like the sun.
Then is the time of his deliverance.

The introduction of the F minor key signature, as it does not conform to the fifth relationship, seems to exclude the possibility of any harmonic continuity with the concluding C♯ of the previous number. However, this number has its own internal coherence through the eventually relatively stable identity of the F minor tonality.

The number begins with a seven-bar introduction in the strings which, with its sustained allegro tempo, generates a sense of momentum. This introduction is repetitive in terms of its rhythmic identity but also in terms of pitch, with its focus on C and B♭ giving it a 'dominant' quality in relation to F minor and paradoxically projecting a sense of harmonic stasis in relation to its rhythmic and temporal mobility. The introduction of the alto solo continues with these features, with the bass line stating a 'dominant' harmony as part of an expanded rhythmic gesture (bar 113: 12). The vocal line also continues with this harmonic and rhythmic gesture, with its first four pitches implying a C-based harmony (C–G–E♭–G). The first point of departure comes in bar 115: 4/5, where the rise from B♭ to E♭ in the lower strings provides a cadential gesture which introduces a new, wind-based texture. Although material derived from the initial gesture, which was defined through its rhythmic shape, continues to dominate, the change from strings to wind – another example of Tippett's fascination with sudden juxtapositions of texture – generates contrast. The change of pitch orientation indicated by the move from B♭ to E♭ in the bass is confirmed by the bassoon part, which now revolves around these pitches. However, the vocal line, beginning at bar 115: 7, contradicts this emphasis with a line which begins on A♭ but concludes with a descent from F♯ to B♮ (bar 115: 9). This now initiates a focus on B in the wind parts, with the bassoon line implying a B harmony. The vocal gesture returns at bar 116: 1, now beginning on A and moving towards G–C; this C, like the previous B, is briefly emphasised.

The wind-based accompaniment continues until bar 117: 2, at which point the brass provide a new texture for the alto soloist. This passage concludes with a G♭ harmony (118: 2) which is followed by a fragmentary intrusion by the strings. The intrusion anticipates the increased involvement of the strings and a greater interaction between the string, wind and brass textures. Bar 118: 2 is marked by a rise from E♭ to B♭ in the alto solo, suggesting a return to prominence for these pitches. However, this B♭, in convergence with the wind texture, forms part of a realisation of the already-mentioned G♭ harmony, and the G♭ does not provide any real stability as it is immediately followed by A (bar 118: 3). Bars 118: 5/6 feature a quasi-cadential gesture formed between B♭ and F, which is repeated on these pitches towards the end of the number with the minor thirds formed between F♯ and A (119: 9) and B and D (figure 120) providing some contrast.

28. Scena

Bass: The words of wisdom are these:
Winter cold means inner warmth, the secret nursery of the seed.

Chorus: How shall we have patience for the consummation of the mystery?
Who will comfort us in the going through?

Bass: Patience is born in the tension of loneliness.
The garden lies beyond the desert.

Chorus: Is the man of destiny master of us all?
Shall those cast out be unavenged?

Bass: The man of destiny is cut off from fellowship.
Healing springs from the womb of time.
The simple-hearted shall exult in the end.

Chorus: What of the boy, then? What of him?

Bass: He, too, is outcast, his manhood broken in the clash of powers.
God overpowered him – the child of our time.

This number is characterised by the juxtaposition of recitative-like vocal writing for the bass solo and quasi-imitative passages for the chorus. The bass solo recalls the passages for the Narrator, as does the initial accompaniment. F♯ is first established as the pitch of the number but it moves quickly towards E in the third bar before this pitch is stated again as the bass of a fuller orchestral texture at bar 121: 2. The melodic prominence of G combines with E in the bass to produce a minor third, and there is also a move from E to B in the bass: a juxtaposition of the minor third and fifth relationships within the short orchestral statement. This idea returns at bar 122: 1 but now the minor third is formed between F♯ in the bass and A in the central part of the melody. However, rather than gravitating towards C♯ and the realisation of the fifth relationship, the statement now concludes on B♭: another example of Tippett's varied repetition.

Between these two points the chorus has a quasi-imitative texture which begins on B (alto and bass) followed by C (soprano and tenor) with both then moving towards A. This arrival on A coincides with the F♯/A element in the orchestra, thus reinforcing its significance. The bass solo returns at bar 123: 1, again with a reduced, somewhat fragmentary accompaniment and a declamatory vocal style which recalls that of the Narrator. Once more the quasi-recitative is interrupted by a contrasting extended orchestral texture leading to the return of the chorus at 124: 4. Again there is a juxtaposition between orchestra and chorus which leads to the return of the bass solo at bar 126: 1. The chorus returns at bar 127: 3 followed by the final appearance of the bass solo. The latter concludes on E but the last two bars of orchestral texture move to A. This A can now be associated retrospectively with the initial F♯ to present a minor-third-based frame for the number: another apposite illustration of the interaction between locally recurring intervals and large-scale motions between the beginning and ends of specific numbers.

29. General Ensemble

Chorus and Soli

Tenor: I would know my shadow and my light,
So shall I at last be whole.
Bass: Then courage, brother, dare the grave passage.
Soprano: Here is no final grieving, but an abiding hope.
Alto: The moving waters renew the earth.
It is spring.

A short instrumental passage, defined in the score as Preludium, introduces the number. It is based on an imitative dialogue between the wind instruments which begins on E♭ and B♭ in the flute parts before descending towards the initial texture of the actual number. Like others in the score, this passage of instrumental imitation is essentially static in function and contemplative in nature.

This extensive number for the quartet of soloists and chorus features a simplification and clarification of certain recurring elements, in particular the repeated pedal effect in the bass which now assumes the appearance of a ground bass. The bass begins on B and, with the new key signature of two sharps, there is a strongly implied B minor tonality. Above this slow-moving texture Tippett presents his final lyrical reflection on the subject matter, with the crucial words of the text, 'I would know my shadow and my light, so shall I at last be whole', initiating a dialogue between the solo voices. The simplified nature of this number is made apparent by the first entry of the chorus (134: 1), which is prepared for by a clear move from F♯ to B in the bass, reasserting the tonality of B minor after an extended repetition of A (133: 1 – 133: 6). Following a more intense period of activity, A is regained in the bass at bar 136: 3 and remains constant to the end of the number. This move from the initial B to the final extended passage on A does not conform to the recurring intervallic dimensions of the work. Nevertheless, it does again represent a sense of movement from beginning to end. But, as a later stage of the discussion will make clear, this does not necessarily imply a functional progression from one pitch centre to another.

As with the move from the soprano solo (No. 7) into 'Steal away' at the conclusion of Part I, Tippett here again attempts to effect a connection to the following spiritual, but now it is the quartet of soloists who are employed in this function. The extended four-part melismatic vocal writing on 'Ah' extends from bar 136: 3 to the end of the number, at which point it does not provide a common-tone link but there is a sense of directed motion. In effect the soprano line falls from D♯ onto G♯ as the first pitch of the spiritual's melody while the bass moves from F♯ to C♯. These intervals create the impression of a cadential motion into the spiritual. In conjunction with these fifth relations, the alto and tenor have semitone motions which are again connected to the spiritual, with the alto moving from C to C♯ and the tenor from A to G♯. While these lines can be interpreted as preparing for the concluding spiritual, the reduction in contrast between the two numbers weakens the dramatic effectiveness of the final spiritual. The transition to 'O, by and by' (No. 25), which raised similar problems, has already been discussed on p. 62 above.

30. A Spiritual

Chorus and Soli
Deep river, my home is over Jordan,
Deep river, Lord,
I want to cross over into camp-ground.

O, chillin! O, don't you want to go,
To that gospel feast,
That promised land,
That land where all is peace?
Walk into heaven, and take my seat,
And cast down my crown at Jesus' feet.

Deep river, my home is over Jordan,
I want to cross over into camp-ground,
Lord!

This concluding spiritual represents the final reconciliation after the events of the previous dramatic narrative. In purely musical terms, it is also a moment of harmonic stasis in contrast to what has come before, although here the contrast is perhaps less clearly marked, since the previous number, with its simplified and clarified sense of harmonic motion, anticipates the stasis of the spiritual.

5

Musical languages

The spirituals

The story of how Tippett became aware of the potential of spirituals has already been told, as has their relationship to the overall design of the work. Tippett's source for the spirituals was a commercially available publication, *The Book of American Negro Spirituals*. Published in 1926, this text reflects how the spiritual was popularly received at that period. The introduction to the volume gives the following commentary on the arrangements, with specific reference to the harmonic vocabulary:

> The songs collected in this book have been arranged for solo voice, but in the piano accompaniments the arrangers have sincerely striven to give the characteristic harmonies that would be used in spontaneous group singing. Of course, these harmonies are not fixed. A group or congregation singing spontaneously might never use precisely the same harmonies twice; however, Mr. Rosamond Johnson and Mr. Brown [the arrangers] have shown great fidelity to what is characteristic. The ordinary four-part harmonies can, without difficulty, be picked out from the accompaniments to most of the songs, but what the arrangers had principally in mind was to have the instrumentation approach the effect of the singing group in action.[1]

> In the arrangements, Mr. Rosamond Johnson and Mr. Brown have been true not only to the best traditions of the melodies but also to form. No changes have been made in the form of songs. The only development has been in harmonizations, and these harmonizations have been kept true in character.[2]

It is difficult to speculate what form this 'development' of the harmony might have assumed. Nevertheless, it does seem to imply some elaboration of a more basic underlying harmonic texture, thus compromising the 'authenticity' of these arrangements. Tippett provides his own description of his approach to harmonising the spiritual:

I had to elevate this musical vernacular to take charge of feelings of a rather higher order without at all losing its immediacy of impact and appeal. This did not just mean purging the conventional harmonies of sentimentality: but rather in apparently excluding all harmonies whatsoever. I accepted the underlying conventional chord of the added seventh particular to each spiritual, and often sought variety only through rhythmic counterpoint and by playing off tonal masses of choral sound against solo-voiced leaders. The harmonically static choruses, thus, at the five critical points, provided a peculiar contrast to the much more harmonically ambiguous music of the other numbers. They became periods of rest.[3]

The static quality of the spirituals and their function as 'periods of rest' in contrast to their surrounding contexts has already emerged in the previous chapter. However, at this stage of the discussion I wish to consider what form 'apparently excluding all harmonies whatsoever' might take. In the view of Bowen, 'Tippett rejected the harmonization of the spirituals in the published versions he had obtained . . .'[4] While it may be difficult to accept the suggestion of a literally complete rejection, Tippett's own statement implies at the very least some reduction between the published source and the final score. This becomes evident from a straightforward comparison between the two. For example, Tippett's setting of 'Go Down Moses' in Part II of the score involves some slight but significant adjustments in the harmony as published in the book. Ex. 5.1a reproduces the Johnson version of the setting of the words 'in Egypt land, Tell old . . .' Tippett's realisation of this part of the text, as reproduced in Ex. 5.1b shows notable differences, with I–IV/IV–I replacing I–I–V^{7c}–I/VI (see Exx. 5.1c and d). Although this may not appear to be a great difference, the removal of the V^{7c}–I progression does result in a simpler harmonic motion and the substitution of VI by IV–I in the next bar perhaps removes some of the alleged 'sentimentality'. The next, perhaps more significant, difference comes in the next bar of the melody ('Pharaoh'). The Johnson version gives a bass line of B moving to B♭ before falling back to C as part of the cadence (Ex. 5.1e). In contrast, Tippett omits the B–B♭ chromatic motion and has a simplified move from F to B♭ followed by the cadential moment on C (Ex. 5.1f).

Ex. 5.1

(a) 'Go down, Moses', arranged by J. Rosamond Johnson

(c)

Tippett's setting of 'Deep river' again shows a number of differences from the source. The Johnson version is (initially) harmonised in E major, which seems somewhat inappropriate for both melody and text, but Tippett's version begins clearly in C♯ minor and features a simplified bass line based on C♯ moving to F♯ (Ex. 5.2a and b). Comparison between the two versions of the initial melodic statement, even allowing for the different tonality, again reflects Tippett's reductive approach to his source. The first version (Ex. 5.2a) features an active bass line with some chromatic inflexion; B♯ in bar 4 leading to C♯, and the A♯ in bar 6 involving a move to the dominant, B. In contrast to this movement, Tippett's version (Ex. 5.2b) involves a simple move between C♯ and G♯ and then F♯ (139), followed by the replacement of a chromatic move from A to A♯–B–C♮–C♯ by a stable A as the root of a IV harmony (139: 2).

Even from these short examples, Tippett's reduction and clarification are quite evident, providing an illumination of Bowen's suggestion of an actual rejection of the 'harmonizations of the spirituals in the published versions . . .'[5]

Ex. 5.1 (*cont.*)

(b) Tippett's setting of 'Go down, Moses'

The issue is further complicated by Tippett's realisation of 'Nobody knows'. The Johnson version (see Ex. 5.3a) consists of simple block-like harmony, giving the impression that this is already in fact a harmonic reduction. In contrast, Tippett's realisation (Ex. 5.3b) is more elaborate. The first, most obvious, difference is rhythmic/metric: Tippett's version halves the note values, reducing the initial sixteen-bar melody into an eight-bar framework; however, the crotchet–minim pattern becomes not literally quaver–crotchet but a faster-moving syncopated quaver pattern (♪♪♪♪♪). The new texture is also more complex in terms of contrapuntal motion, with a dialogue within the choral parts projected against the tenor solo, and an initial pattern of imitation within the accompaniment following that of the choral parts. Although the under-

Ex. 5.1 (*cont.*)

(e)

(f)

lying harmonies remain similar between the two versions, Tippett's adaptation is now also rendered more harmonically complex as a consequence of the contrapuntal texture.

In considering Tippett's adaptations of the spirituals, the question of texture becomes as significant as the discussion of the harmonic process. Following his comments concerning the use of the published

Ex. 5.2

(a) 'Deep river', arranged by J. Rosamond Johnson

Ex. 5.2 (*cont.*)
(b) Tippett's setting of 'Deep river'

Ex. 5.3

(a) 'Nobody knows', arranged by J. Rosamond Johnson

collection of spirituals, Tippett discusses their presentation in performance:

> The next question, that of presentation, meant a further purchase from America: this time recordings of a cappella performances of spirituals by the relatively conventional Hal [Hall] Johnson Choir (whom I remembered from the sound-track of the film *Green Pastures*) and by the 'hot' vocal group called the Mitchell Christian Singers. These latter went in for cross-rhythmical counterpoint by the spoken voice, as well as a great deal of blues-provoked ambiguity of pitch. Fascinating though this disc was, I had to forego [*sic*] such extreme methods of presentation, if only for the sake of the normal European concert-hall choir. I also realised that I would have to purify the harmonies and clarify the contrapuntal texture.[6]

While the problems involved in Tippett's need to 'purify the harmonies and clarify the contrapuntal texture' have already been indicated, his hearing of the Hall Johnson Choir provided him with textures which helped to shape the relationship between soloist and choir. After stating that Tippett 'rejected the harmonization of the spirituals he had

Ex. 5.3 (*cont.*)

(b) Tippett's setting of 'Nobody knows'

obtained', Bowen goes on to suggest that he 're-worked them so as to pit the soloists dramatically against the chorus. This technique he learnt from the singing of the Hall Johnson Choir on the soundtrack to *Green Pastures*.'[7]

Tippett's writing for soloists against a choral background in the spirituals results in some of the most effective moments in the work. For example, the realisation of 'Steal away' provides a dramatic transition, which has already been referred to in chapter 4, through the use of the soprano solo. But what specifically Tippett takes from the tradition of performance as he experienced it, is the use of the soloist, in 'Steal away' the tenor, to effectively 'lead' the vocal ensemble. At bar 60: 4 the tenor solo is projected in a declamatory style before the choir re-enters the texture in response to the soloist. Within the full choral passages in this spiritual the tenor soloist is still present, and is joined by the return of the soprano soloist at the effective high point of the texture.

The idea of a dialogue between soloist and chorus is most evident in 'Go down Moses'. The entry of the bass soloist at bar 93: 1 comes after a uniform and somewhat static choral texture, thereby gaining in dramatic significance. The final spiritual, 'Deep river', also features a notable contrast of texture between soloists and chorus. In this instance the chorus presents a consistent flowing texture to which the soloists' interjections add dramatic poignancy.

Thematic/motivic connections

Important though the origins and identity of the spirituals are, more significant are the questions which have continued to surround the relationship of the spirituals to the work as a whole, questions that will be seen to form a recurring pattern within the early reception of the work. In his essay 'What Do We Perceive in Modern Art?', published as part of *Moving into Aquarius*, Tippett directly confronts this critical perspective:

> I mention those criticisms pointed at my using Negro spirituals within such an apparently sophisticated score. Here I think we can see that the original incompatibility of emotionally complex composed music and popularly derived simple melody, if set side by side, without mediation, leads critics into a prejudice at first hearing, which could not be overcome

until the mediatory process . . . is understood. It is perhaps analogous to the shocks people first had at being presented with the mixture of sophisticated and popular in the poems of W. H. Auden. The passage of time has uncovered the poetic connections. So it has done with the musical connections of *A Child of Our Time*. The transitions from composed music to the settings of the spirituals are now accepted as one of the achievements of the piece.[8]

While some of the 'transitions' from composed music to the settings of the spirituals are certainly musically effective, questions must remain concerning both the nature and extent of the integration. The central issue that comes from this extended quotation is that of mediation. Within this particular essay Tippett does not clarify what actual shape or form this process of mediation might take. However, writing in a different context, he returns to the issue and provides some insight into how one might attempt to mediate between, and by implication reconcile, what are essentially two distinct sound worlds:

I had to accept . . . that [the] virtue of emotional release supplied by the spirituals had to be paid for by allowing the popular words and music to affect the *general* style, within which the 'sophisticated' parts of the oratorio had to be written. I used the interval of a minor third, produced so characteristically in the melodies of the spirituals when moving from the fifth of the tonic to the flat seventh, as a basic interval for the whole work . . .[9]

This suggestion of a specific interval, the minor third, being extracted from the idiom of the spiritual and extended into the surrounding musical contexts is explored in some detail by Kemp, who suggests that shared intervals combine to form a 'common ground' between the two sound worlds. Ex. 5.4 is derived from Kemp's outline of this intervallic process. The starting point is the melodic line of the spiritual 'Nobody knows' (Ex. 5.4a, Kemp's Ex. 46), which, as highlighted in chapter 3, is placed as the effective centre of the work. The minor third formed through the descent from B♭ to G is identified as *a*, to which Kemp adds the initial rising fifth formed between C and G (identified as *b*) and the fall of a seventh from B♭ to C (identified as *c*), identifying these elements as potentially significant. Ex. 5.4b, which reproduces part of Kemp's Ex. 47(i), consists of a reduction of the orchestral texture of the opening moments of the score. Identified as *b* is the linear descent from B as part

Ex. 5.4

(a)

[Kemp, p. 165, Ex. 46]

(b)

[Kemp, p. 166, Ex. 47 (i)]

(i)

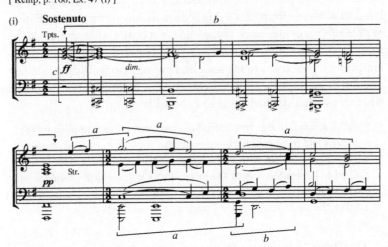

(ii)

of the initial E minor sonority to E. Following this descending fifth, Kemp identifies the importance of the minor third, with the rise from E to G followed by the descent from D to B in the upper part and a bass motion also from E to G being evident. According to Kemp, this example 'illustrates Tippett's resource in deriving a variety of motivic beginnings from these three intervals. His method ranges from the relatively straightforward use of the minor third . . . to more subtle usages in which the interval is regarded as a musical space to be filled out or expanded and developed as a chromatic motif. The same method is applied throughout the rest of the oratorio.'[10] The prevalence of the minor third and the recurring significance of the fifth were clearly evident in the previous chapter and these intervals are, as filtered through Kemp's brief analysis, the implied process of mediation between the sound world of the spiritual and that of Tippett himself. But is this mediation strong and effective enough to enable the work to achieve the unified status implied by both Tippett's own comments and Kemp's brief analytical outline?[11]

Depending on one's theoretical assumptions and their originating aesthetic ideology, recurring intervals as motivic connection can be interpreted either as the substance that integrates two sound worlds or merely as a sequence of fragments that are translated from one context into another without necessarily unifying the two. It is clear, as I have already stated, that for both Tippett and Kemp unity is achieved. However, this basic interpretation does not take account of the fact that the materials which define the two sound worlds are predicated on two very different musical idioms and to assume unification on the basis of some shared intervallic characteristics may be somewhat optimistic. In the process of the transference of the minor third from one sound world into another, the interval leaves behind the explicitly diatonic language of the spiritual and is often effectively redefined in a new harmonic context some distance away from it. This is already evident from the musical contexts from which these examples (5.4a and b) are extracted. The construction of a Schenkerian voice-leading graph for the spiritual 'Nobody knows' would be an extremely unproblematic exercise, consisting as it does of a simple unfolding of its C minor tonality, whereas the work's initial material is clearly resistant to such a definition.

Further consideration of Ex. 5.4b indicates that the musical language of this passage is not only some distance from that of the uncomplicated diatonicism of the spiritual, but also predicated on an often uneasy tension between the chromatic and diatonic, described by Whittall as a 'disconcerting shift from chromatic to diatonic and back again'.[12] As a consequence of this 'disconcerting shift', the passage is rendered unstable in relation to its implied tonality. The initial E minor sonority is seemingly contradicted by the descending chromatic bass line, a shift which is expanded upon throughout this opening section. Also of significance is the fact that the arrival of the linear melodic descent on E coincides not with an E minor tonic but with a relatively unstable harmony (F♯–A–C–E, Kemp's c).

The brief comparison between 'Nobody knows' and the work's opening bars reveals the sense of distance between them, a sense of distance that renders the construction of a process of mediation through the deployment of a recurring interval inherently problematic.

Tonal structure: harmonic unity or polarity?

Throughout the synopsis of the musical details in chapter 4 reference was made to the ongoing significance of the fifth relationship, to such an extent that it would seem that this recurring element has a potentially wider structural and/or harmonic function. According to Kemp, 'As a final means of imposing unity on the work Tippett designed a tonal structure of considerable subtlety.'[13] This tonal structure is essentially defined through a sequence of fifth-related pitch centres. Kemp relates this to 'a kind of progressive tonality'.[14] However, further consideration of, for example, the opening moments of the work suggests that it is difficult to trace how this process actually unfolds as a 'progression'. As Ex. 4.1 demonstrated, the number is defined through the juxtaposition of sustained pitch centres of E and B, with the final move to B coming not as the result of a progression but as the final shift in the ongoing juxtaposition of these two pitches. This juxtaposition then can be seen as the defining harmonic characteristic, a characteristic that allows us to begin to interpret Tippett's harmonic language in relation to Stravinsky's metaphor of polarity and to a wider neoclassical practice.

Writing in his *Poetics of Music*, Stravinsky made the following, much discussed statement:

our chief concern is not so much what is known as tonality as what one might term the polar attraction of sound, of an interval, or even a complex of tones . . . All music being nothing but a succession of impulses and repose, it is easy to see that the drawing together and separation of poles of attraction in a way determine the respiration of music.

In view of the fact that our poles of attraction are no longer within the closed system which was the diatonic system, we can bring the poles together without being compelled to conform to the exigencies of tonality.[15]

The wide-ranging implications of this statement have been interpreted from several different angles.[16] Within the immediate context of this work we can conceive of the shift between fifth-related pitches as reflecting 'the polar attraction of sound, of an interval . . .', with each of the two elements providing a source of attraction which focuses the music without necessarily functioning in a way that is reminiscent of a conventional tonic. This notion of polarity through juxtaposition is clearly active in other parts of the score although it will always be realised in different ways. For example, the third number from part 1 (Scena) involves the same two salient pitches as in the opening number but in a perhaps more overt tonal orientation, with the initial B harmony implying a dominant relationship to the indicated tonality of E minor, and it is significant that these two pitches (B–E) return as the concluding cadential gesture of the number. However, while it would be possible to interpret these two pitches as being in a traditional dominant–tonic relationship, the absence of progression and development between them makes it more difficult to sustain such a definition, particularly as the texture is essentially linear. In contrast, it is preferable to suggest that the initial and concluding pitches simply frame the number and, rather than having any meaningful sense of progression, the material is conditioned through the juxtaposition of these two pitches. The idea of polarity is again evident in the soprano solo (No. 23) from Part II. The initial linear unfolding of B minor in the lower strings provides a degree of focus on B (bars 98: 7 – 99: 4), which is eventually juxtaposed with the final affirmation of F♯ (bars 103: 4 – 103: 11). This relationship could be framed within the tonal context of B minor, but it is significant that this fifth relationship is also echoed by the move from D to G (100: 1 – 100: 4) and that there is no real sense of a linear/harmonic progression from beginning to end. The associated issues of juxtaposition and beginning–end relationships emerge through the discussion of several individual numbers, to such an extent that polarity can now be viewed as the underlying formal/harmonic principle of the work.

However, it is still possible to suggest a degree of large-scale continuity across these salient pitch-class centres. This is certainly the case in Part I of the score. The initial shift between E and B in the opening chorus section is mirrored in the third number (Scena) by a move back to E from B. This larger alternation can associate with G as the final pitch centre of Part I, a centre which was anticipated in the sixth number and further defined in the seventh and eighth. These focal points outline the E minor triad and reflect the significance of the minor third and perfect fifth as defined by Kemp.

This triadic outline can be interpreted as a 'background structure' for the entirety of Part I, but given that it is defined through juxtaposition it is difficult to conceive of the pattern as being generative in relation to the localised detail. In Part III of the work the large-scale fifth relationship consists of a shift from the initial F♯ to the final realisation of C♯, a process that has been anticipated in the opening chorus of this final part of the score. Also of significance is the shift from F♯ to A in the Scena (No. 28), with A again providing the final pitch centre of the General Ensemble (No. 29). This focus on A then completes the central point of an extended linear realisation of the triad of F♯ minor, with the other pitch centres being seen as secondary to this pattern.[17] The F♯ minor triad can be seen as a transposition of the E minor of Part I:

Part I	Part III
E	F♯
G	A
B	C♯

The central section, Part II, seems to depart this principle: as a consequence of its extended nature and the number of harmonically unfocused passages, particularly those of the Narrator (Nos. 10, 12, 14, 18, 20), it is at times difficult to perceive longer-term patterns. Although the fifth relationship is again established between the first and final pitch centres, D and A, the required F is avoided for much of the time, with F♯

seeming to have a greater degree of significance, particularly as it forms the final pitch centre of the opening chorus of Part II (No. 9). Nevertheless, F functions as the tonic of the strategically positioned spiritual 'Go down Moses'(No. 21), producing the following pattern:

9	21	25
Chorus	Spiritual	Spiritual
'A star rises in mid winter . . .'	Go down Moses	O by and by
D	F	A

This clarification now opens up the possibility of interpreting the minor third, in association with the fifth-based relationship, as providing a 'background' for the work as a whole:

Part I
E ——— G ——— B

Part II
D ——— F ——— A

Part III
F♯——— A ——— C♯

However, if this linear pattern is interpreted as a 'background' to the work as a whole, then it is difficult to define its relationship to the more localised musical details. Clearly there are detailed reflections of the fifth-related polarities and minor third relationships within what could be understood as the surface of the music, a factor which clearly emerged through the analysis in chapter 4. For example, the significance of the fifth relationship identified in Ex. 4.1 can connect with the larger process, with the juxtaposition of linear presentations of the minor third (Kemp's *a*), formed through the rise from E to G and the following descent from D to B, combining to construct a realisation of both the minor third and fifth relationships (see Ex. 5.4b). But it is difficult to conceive of these reflections as being controlled through the operations of a background structure.

The problems of defining this large-scale intervallic pattern are reinforced by the textural discontinuity which, as emerged in the previous chapter, is a defining characteristic of the work. It is difficult to conceive of a device that could take such a diverse range of musical materials – the extended fugal choruses, the expansive writing for the solo voices, the spirituals and the recitative textures for the Narrator – and subsume these diversities under a single unifying principle.

This discussion brings the focus back to Tippett's relationship to the work of T. S. Eliot, which was first discussed in chapter 2, with the suggestion that Eliot provided a source of influence beyond just the text itself. It is clear that Eliot's poetic language as manifested in *The Waste Land* often shifts uneasily between unity and fragmentation. But in many interpretations of this epic poem the framework of a consistent mythology emerges, and it is against this mythology that the fragmentary poetic images and allusions are projected. According to Jewel Spears Brooker,

> An essential part of Eliot's approach to form in *The Waste Land* is his appropriation of a specific myth as a reference point. The myth of choice, Frazer's Ur-myth, is privileged by its presentation as the original myth from which all others descended and from which all others evolved into fragments; it is privileged by its prior-ity in time and its total comprehensiveness.[18]

On a purely musical level, I suspect that a similar process occurs in *A Child of Our Time*, with the 'background' process outlined above giving it a coherence through which it becomes possible to make sense of the fragmentary materials and juxtapositions, but that the coherence that emerges from this process stops some way short of an actual unified structure.

6

Reception

A Child of Our Time was first performed at the Adelphi Theatre,
London, on 19 March 1944. Walter Goehr conducted the London Phil-
harmonic Orchestra, the London Region Civil Defence Choir and
Morley College Choir, with the solo parts sung by Joan Cross, Margaret
McArthur, Peter Pears and Roderick Lloyd. The success of this performance, coming three years after the completion of the work (a delay
which was partly due to the war-time conditions), signified the emergence of Tippett as a mature composer now able to begin to connect with
a wider public. Benjamin Britten was central to this first performance as
it was his encouragement which gave Tippett the confidence he needed.
Following a description of their shared interest in Purcell, Tippett
recalls Britten's involvement:

> Ben . . . asked me what larger works I had written, if any, other than those
> he knew. I told him of *A Child of Our Time*, of how I had played it to Walter
> Goehr some time before, who advised me in the circumstances to shut it
> up in a drawer, which, being rather patient and literal, I did. Ben had the
> manuscript out of the drawer at once. In looking through the score, he
> noticed how, in one of the spirituals, the effect could be greatly enhanced
> by lifting the tenor solo part suddenly an octave higher. This I entirely
> agreed with, and so this minute piece of Britten composition is in the
> score. He persuaded us to venture to a performance; he was already then
> close to Sadler's Wells Opera, and talked three of their singers into singing
> for us: Joan Cross, Peter Pears, and Roderick Lloyd. The fourth, Margaret
> McArthur, came from us at Morley. In the event, through no fault of these
> artists, it was an imperfect premiere under execrable conditions, but ines-
> capably moving.[1]

The first written response to the work came from John Amis in a short
article published in *The Musical Times* in February 1944. This article

functioned as a preface to the forthcoming performance and outlines many of the main features of the work. As Amis also sought to introduce the composer to a wider public, his tone is obviously uncritical, concluding with a prediction of success and continuing significance for it:

> The general style of the oratorio is simple and direct, and the music will, I think, have an immediate effect on both audience and performers. The first performance on March 19 at the Adelphi theatre may well be a noteworthy event in which once more a new English oratorio is brought before the public. It is a work which I have little hesitation in recommending to the more enterprising of our national choirs.[2]

Following the first performance, the initial critical response was largely favourable, with the most interesting early published reaction coming from Edwin Evans. Writing in *The Musical Times*, he described it as 'one of the major events of music in wartime'. However, he goes on in a more critical vein:

> The effect of the whole work is arresting, absorbing. Yet one wonders at moments whether it really reflects the text. In its very simplicity this seems to aim at kindling a noble indignation, a passionate resentment, but the music is, generally speaking, too intellectual to express strong emotions of that nature.

This question of the music's inability to truly reflect the text was to become a recurring issue in the reception of both this work in particular and Tippett's subsequent text-based works in general, with the humanitarian concerns of the text and the alleged intellectual rigour of the formal musical processes at times being seen as coexisting within a basic discontinuity.

It is true that Evans goes on in a more positive mode, stating that 'Apart from that the oratorio is a remarkably fine work, original in conception and transparently sincere in realization, and its performance might easily become a landmark in the history of the form.' But this positive response is again further qualified by his comments concerning the position and significance of the spirituals. After considering their symbolic nature, he goes on to conclude that 'they do not add to its expressiveness, as the peculiar poignancy they have in their traditional form tends to evaporate in their new environment'.[3] Once again, this statement anticipates a critical trend: the status and function of the spirituals and the problem of their integration into the surrounding musical context became a continuous feature of writings on the work. However, *The Musical Times* for the following month (May 1944) featured a review of the score which functioned as a footnote to both Amis's article and the review of the first performance. Written by William McNaught, this short review contains an unreservedly positive view of the spirituals:

> The use of Negro spirituals in the manner of chorales has been remarked upon as a curiosity, or even as a self-conscious oddity. Close examination of the work acquits the composer of any such insincerity. The idea that a spiritual must be out of place arises from the cloying harmony and senti-mentality in which such things are commonly dressed for our amusement, and from their false association with quaintness and comedy. Mr. Tippett divests them of these unrealities and brings them into harmony with his text – a harmony that is both technical and expressive.[4]

This highly affirmative response, claiming a perfect synthesis between music and text, effectively endorses the composer's understanding of his own work.

Eric Blom, in a review of the published score prior to the first performance, presents a more qualified view. He begins with the assertion that 'This is a very remarkable work treating a subject urgently concerning the salvation of present-day humanity as if it were matter for a classical oratorio.' But, again, questions concerning the spirituals are raised:

> The general design of [the] three parts loosely resembles that of Handel's 'Messiah', and so does the composer's division of the text into recitatives, arias and choruses; but he also makes use of popular tunes very much as Bach does of the chorales in his Passions, and it is significant that these tunes are those which voice the emotional aspirations of a minority race – Negro spirituals. The idea is brilliant and the analogy with Bach's practice convincing in Mr. Tippett's theory. All the same there is a difference. Bach's own style was largely formed on the chorale; Mr. Tippett's own manner, which is spare, linear and unsentimental in its most copious aspects, will not let the luscious Negro tunes, which cry out for an opulent harmonic treatment, become integrated with it.

This statement can now be interpreted as very perceptive. The question of the integration of the spiritual material, as already suggested, forms the central issue in most subsequent discussions of the music. But the distinction that Blom makes between the example of Bach and Tippett is revealing; Bach's use of the chorale was contained within his own musical and cultural horizons whereas Tippett is attempting to transfer, perhaps translate, a musical idiom which lies outside his own context, producing a certain degree of dislocation between the two. As well as raising these questions concerning the spirituals, Blom also goes on to question the nature and validity of Tippett's text: 'It is tempting to mention some interesting technical features, so far as the vocal score reveals them. The words are very terse and bald – rather poor really, but the composer-author may be expected to counter that criticism by the assertion that they were meant to be so . . .'[5] Again, as with Evans's comments, this statement anticipates a certain critical view of Tippett's own texts, a view which would come to manifest itself in relation to the operas.

However, it is once more the question of the nature of the integration of the spirituals which is most stridently addressed by R. J. Manning. Writing in *The Monthly Musical Record* in October 1945, he provides the following critical overview:

> As the spirituals have aroused very different responses in the breasts of the various music critics, it is worth examining in some detail the part they play in the work. Tippett himself says: 'Bach took the material for his chorales from the current collections of the day to suit the emotional situations of his oratorios. I will use the universal songs of the present time that most nearly correspond to the situations in my own oratorio'. But are the Negro spirituals so universal?

Manning goes on to question Tippett's understanding of the universal significance of the spiritual, arguing that their importance is specific to a certain context; and he compares this context to a more specifically English one. He concludes: 'I am convinced that much of the audience's enthusiasm for the work was due to these spirituals, simply because they are beautiful songs in themselves. One would be dull indeed not to be moved by them. But they detract from the unity of the work.'[6] It is significant that Manning's main criticism is not so much what he considers as Tippett's mistaken understanding of the symbolic nature of the spirituals but the fact that their inclusion undermines the musical unity of the work and thus challenges preconceptions concerning the nature of musical form.

Thus although all these initial responses share a certain positive attitude towards the work, more critical issues such as the viability of the text and the integration of the spirituals are also clearly brought into focus. However, even this qualified enthusiasm is avoided by Colin Mason. In one of the first general overviews of Tippett's music, published in 1946, he stated: 'Considered as a whole, Tippett's choral works are as yet insufficient in quantity or distinction to be really important. It is for his instrumental works that he ranks so high.'[7] Although this statement does not in itself refer directly to *A Child of Our Time*, it can only be read in relation to it. Mason's statement not only remains a somewhat odd conclusion given the central position of *A Child of Our Time* within Tippett's development, it also fails to take account of his struggle to master large-scale forms within the earlier instrumental works.

In terms of popular perception *A Child of Our Time* has maintained its place in the repertoire and has enjoyed several successful recordings. However, from the point of view of informed scholarship the work remains largely untouched, a problem it shares with Tippett's music in general. Writing in 1989, David Clarke offered the following overview of the existing literature on Tippett and his music:

> The recognition accorded to Michael Tippett in recent years as one of the greatest of a senior generation of composers has been matched by an increase in the amount of literature written about him. In general this must be greeted positively as a sign of widespread interest in his music, and as a stimulus to critical debate. At the same time, however, we should note that the proportion of these writings devoted to a deeper investigation of what is, after all, the main source of interest, the music itself, is disappointingly small. Of six books published around and between Tippett's 75th and 80th birthdays three – by Eric Walter White, David Matthews and Meirion Bowen – are introductory studies, and – reasonably enough – afford only limited space to discussion of individual works. The most recent publication, a compilation edited by Geraint Lewis, entitled *Michael Tippett O.M.: A Celebration*, offers a fairly representative sample of the type and quality of shorter writings to which we have grown accustomed.[8]

Since Clarke made this statement the situation has improved somewhat, partly through his own efforts, but the position, given the quantity of more accessible commentary on Tippett's work and his status, remains far from ideal. The two books which Clarke goes on to refer to in a more positive light, Ian Kemp's *Tippett: The Composer and His Music* and Arnold Whittall's *The Music of Britten and Tippett: Studies in Themes and Techniques*, both of which have been referred to throughout this book, are clearly still the only central reference points for a general understanding of Tippett's music, as well as the only useful source of more detailed commentary on specific works.

It is interesting to note that Kemp and Whittall continue to sustain the debate surrounding the integration of the spirituals and come to very different and distinctive conclusions. According to Kemp:

> *A Child of Our Time* showed that Tippett had acquired a highly developed control of dramatic gesture and pacing, a distinctive vocal and choral style and an ability to dispose unifying techniques over a wide canvas. Such technical advances cannot of course create genuine artistic unity by themselves. But the work does have a unity, nowhere more evident than in those passages where it is most threatened, the transitions from Tippett's 'own' music to that of the spirituals.[9]

This view of the work as ultimately unifying itself was touched upon in relation to the construction of the text and was explored again, more critically, through the examination of specific musical details, particularly the transitions between the spirituals and Tippett's 'own' material in chapter 5. At this stage in the discussion it is sufficient to note the assumptions of unity and integration upon which Kemp's interpretation is based. In contrast to this view, Whittall claims: 'a note in the score of *A Child of Our Time* declares that "the spirituals should not be thought of as congregational hymns, but as integral parts of the oratorio". That is perhaps the problem: they are not integral enough . . .'[10] Writing in another context, Whittall returns to this issue:

> Of all Tippett's earlier works, it is perhaps *A Child of Our Time* which conveys the least unified impression, but there is no evidence that the composer sought deliberately to portray contemporary social and political tensions by means of a '*Merzbild*'[11] created from the juxtaposition and superimposition of diverse musics, as he might have, for example, from a 'random' polyphony of Negro Spirituals, or the effect of different Spirituals approaching and passing and receding like Ivesian marches. More realistically, the possibility for unmediated confrontation between the Spirituals and Tippett's own style of the time is positively avoided, for the

obvious reason that the theme of the work is the need for reconciliation: the shadow and the light form the whole.[12]

It is intriguing to speculate as to how the work could have sounded had Tippett followed through the logic of the disparity between his main musical sources into a large-scale collage effect. The resulting work might have portrayed its own historical time more accurately, but, as Whittall indicates, Tippett's main concern was the symbolic desire for reconciliation. This question of the possible reconciliation between the spirituals and Tippett's 'own' music is dramatised through the differing views of Whittall and Kemp, a difference that we can now see as having its origins in the initial critical reception of the work.

7

Legacy

It is possible to situate *A Child of Our Time* – particularly in its relationship to the generic conventions of the oratorio – within a continuing, specifically English, choral tradition. However, any attempt to connect specific aspects of Tippett's work with the high points of that tradition, as defined through oratorios such as Elgar's *Dream of Gerontius* (1899–1900) and Walton's *Belshazzar's Feast* (1930–1), or even such works as Vaughan Williams's *Sea Symphony* (1903–9) or Delius's *Sea Drift* (1903–4), remains an elusive pursuit. If it is difficult to trace precise musical precedents, the extra-musical content of Tippett's work also resists categorisation within the English choral tradition. Even a work as evocative in its subject matter as Bliss's *Morning Heroes* (1930), whose concerns share some common ground with *A Child of Our Time*, cannot be seen to provide any direct precedent for Tippett's work.

If tracing potential precursors for *A Child of Our Time* within the English choral tradition is difficult, any attempt to trace its influence on areas outside Tippett's own stylistic development is equally problematic. Within this immediate context, however, it is clear that the emergent ability to fashion his own texts would have great significance, most obviously in relation to his development as a composer of operas – a development that was to come to fruition in *The Midsummer Marriage* (1946–52), his first opera and a work which best reflects his compositional and aesthetic concerns of the period.

However, although certain characteristics may originate from *A Child of Our Time*, this does not indicate that a direct line of works follows it, either in terms of Tippett's own *œuvre* or within the subsequent historical development of British choral music. According to Stephen Banfield,

The line of committed oratorio, from *A Child of Our Time* to Michael Berkeley's *Or Shall We Die ?* (1983), is not a broad one, though if the *War Requiem* is included it passes at least one high point. Tippett himself has not returned to it, writing his sense of social solidarity instead into his later operas and the Third Symphony, though he has, almost uniquely among front-rank British composers, kept faith with oratorio as a metasymphonic genre, in both *The Vision of St Augustine* (1965) and *The Mask of Time* (1982).[1]

The reference to Britten's *War Requiem* (1958–61) is intriguing. There are certainly some parallels between Tippett's and Britten's use of the large-scale vocal context as a means of making a shared public, pacifist statement. However, it is the requiem mass rather than the oratorio to which Britten makes his generic allusions, and the sound worlds of the two composers are too personal and distinct to enable any meaningful comparison to emerge beyond the obvious shared concerns of the actual subject matter.

Nevertheless, there is, as Banfield suggests, a certain path from *A Child of Our Time* to two important works from later stages in Tippett's stylistic development. Composed between 1963 and 1965, *The Vision of St Augustine* represents Tippett's first large-scale vocal work after *A Child of Our Time*. Given the success of the earlier work it seems somewhat surprising that Tippett waited so long before returning to this musical and literary context. The delay can be partly explained through the focus on opera, a focus that not only consumed Tippett's literary interests but also, especially in *The Midsummer Marriage*, still involved him in writing a great deal for the chorus. Nevertheless, this absence also partly reflects the uniqueness of *A Child of Our Time*, with the resulting gap perhaps emerging as a consequence of both the individuality and success of the earlier oratorio.

The Vision of St Augustine differs from *A Child of Our Time* in a number of important ways, the most obvious being the text. This work represents Tippett's first large-scale attempt to utilise existing texts in preference to constructing his own. The main point of contact with *A Child of Our Time* is formed by Tippett's relationship to Eliot, with allusion and juxtaposition again in evidence. The first direct reference to Eliot is the use of an epigraph from *Burnt Norton*, 'and all is always now'. That this epigraph is taken from *Four Quartets* is in itself notable, as this text resonates with Eliot's Christian symbolism and thus obviously connects with the subject matter of Tippett's work, but it also invokes notions of temporality, which become apparent within the musical dimension.

However, what most clearly emerges again from the relationship to Eliot is, as already suggested, the importance of allusion, a quality that is already active in the text. Arnold Whittall describes the selections of the text:

> The principal portions of text are taken from the later stages of book IX of the *Confessions* – chapters 10 to 14. For Part I the solo baritone is allotted the first paragraph of chapter 10. In itself, this is already allusive, in that it contains three biblical quotations, but in Tippett's structure it forms a background which flowers into a rich complexity as the chorus provide an overlapping commentary, sometimes amplifying the information given by the baritone with lines from elsewhere in the *Confessions*, from the Hymn of Bishop Ambrose (as quoted in the *Confessions*), or from the Bible – the song of Solomon, the Psalms.[2]

However, the allusive practice of this work is a great deal more subtle than that of *A Child of Our Time*, and, although there are many echoes of previous musical styles and gestures, there is little sense of the direct intertextual practices of *A Child of Our Time*.

Although there are inevitable overlaps between the two works there are also significant differences. For example, in contrast to *A Child of Our Time*, there is greater concern with continuity. This continuity is predicated upon repetition, a quality that relates back to Eliot and in particular *Four Quartets*, a work which constructs a cyclic identity through processes of repetition and recapitulation. According to Jewel Spears Brooker, 'In *Four Quartets*, Eliot advances a different method [in comparison to *The Waste Land*], one based on repetition and relation-in-itself rather than on juxtaposition and reconstruction . . .'[3] However, although repetition does replace the juxtapositions of *A Child of Our Time*, it was already evident as an important quality in the earlier work. Throughout chapter 4, reference was made to this quality. For example, Tippett's liking for points of repetition in combination with slight variation, a process that alludes to the conventional gesture of sequence, was evident throughout the score. Nevertheless, in *The Vision* repetition is elevated to new levels of significance through the construction of a more complex image of musical temporality, one that involves a greater, more subtle interaction between continuity and discontinuity than was evident in *A Child of Our Time*. As Whittall suggests, 'There are recurrences, resemblances which reinforce the awareness of something passing through time.'[4] This awareness is generated by the return of certain large-scale passages and also by the recalling of the baritone solo. Whittall provides an effective summary of this process:

> On the large scale, the work is integrated by several substantial passages of 'recapitulation', but the more immediate continuity provided by the 'retakes' of the baritone line – in contrast to the self-contained statements of the chorus – provide the essential structural propulsion of the work. Continuity is further increased by the extent to which the musical material now overlaps the carefully graded contrasts of tempo which is another technical feature carried over from *King Priam* and its successors.[5]

These qualities also become evident again in *The Mask of Time* (1982), a work which revisits some of the concerns of *A Child of Our Time*, but within a context which is shaped by the stylistic concerns of Tippett's later period. The composer provides his own description:

> My composition at best offered fragments, or scenes, from a possible 'epiphany' for today: hence the heterogeneity of the musical conception, which is written 'for voices and instruments'. It is a pageant of sorts: hence the 'Mask' of the title, used in the tradition of the Renaissance masque, which was a theatrical form with a great diversity of ingredients, a mixture of formality and flexibility, and an ultimately lofty message; by using the alternative spelling 'Mask', I deliberately suggested a contemporary ironic ambiguity.[6]

What is most notable in this work is that, from a perspective formed through the later stages of his career, Tippett positively embraces the fragmented nature of his musical materials. Whereas in *A Child of Our Time* he attempted to mediate between his disparate materials and impose an artificial notion of unity upon them, in *The Mask of Time* he now accepts fragmentation as the consequence of the intertextual allusions and extra-musical aspirations. That Tippett came to this position reflects his own changing perception of the world that surrounded him and, in many different ways, shaped his compositional outlook in the two works. And yet these works do have something in common. That Tippett still, at this late stage in his career, wanted to make a bold public statement of his personal vision, to make clear his reaction to the changing world, recalls the basic humanity and sincerity of *A Child of Our Time*. It is perhaps fitting that these two large-scale choral works – one which marked his emergence as a distinctive compositional voice and one which looks back upon his own development – provide a loosely defined boundary to his career, a career which in endlessly divergent contexts continued to restate the individuality of vision first clearly articulated in *A Child of Our Time*.

Notes

Introduction

1 For specific discussions of these works see Arnold Whittall, *The Music of Britten and Tippett: Studies in Themes and Techniques* (Cambridge, 1990), pp. 31–6 and Ian Kemp, *Tippett: The Composer and his Music* (London, 1984), pp. 118–49.

2 Michael Worton and Judith Still (eds.), *Intertextuality: Theories and Practices* (Manchester, 1990), pp. 1–2. The reference to Kristeva is based on her essay 'Word, Dialogue and Novel', in Toril Moi (ed.), *The Kristeva Reader* (Oxford, 1986).

1 Background

1 Meirion Bowen (ed.), *Tippett on Music* (Oxford, 1995), p. 282.

2 Michael Tippett, *Those Twentieth Century Blues* (London, 1994), p. 48. Kemp provides a useful overview of Tippett's political concerns of the 1930s as well as a more detailed description of *War Ramp*. See Kemp, *Tippett*, pp. 25–39.

3 Tippett, *Those Twentieth Century Blues*, p. 46.

4 *Ibid.*, pp. 49–50.

5 Quoted in Maurice Edelman, 'A Composer Listens to his own Oratorio', *Picture Post*, 3 March 1945, p. 19.

6 However, Meirion Bowen does make some attempt to find a point of convergence between the two works:

> If the text is thus rich and multi-layered, so almost deceptively is the music. Its sustained directness and limpid simplicity were qualities Tippett tried to emulate from Berlioz's *L' Enfance du Christ* (which he heard on the radio at the time). The choral and orchestral writing are both distinctive and unusual. Tippett's consistently linear approach, the fruit of his interest in Renaissance music, is evident throughout, and heavyweight performances can easily undermine the impact of the tensions engendered by the flow and clash of lines. The

linking interludes in Nos. 3 and the preludium before no. 29, again challenge the canonically imitative flutes and viola to float their lines across the bar lines: and here the harmonic movement against a sustained B♭ on the cellos is implied rather than overt (as in the 'open', transparent textures encountered so often in Berlioz). (Meirion Bowen, *Michael Tippett* (London, 1997), pp. 89–90)

7 Alan Bullock, *Hitler and Stalin: Parallel Lives* (London, 1993), p. 637.
8 Tippett, *Those Twentieth Century Blues*, p. 110.

2 The text

1 T. S. Eliot, 'Tradition and the Individual Talent', first published in the *Egoist*, September and December 1919, reprinted in Frank Kermode (ed.), *Selected Prose of T. S. Eliot* (London, 1975), pp. 37–44. For a wider discussion of Tippett's relationship to Eliot, see Suzanne Robinson, 'The Pattern from the Palimpsest: The Influence of T. S. Eliot on Michael Tippett', Ph.D. thesis, University of Melbourne (1990).
2 For Tippett's own comments on the importance of Purcell, see Bowen (ed.), *Tippett on Music*, pp. 57–65.
3 *Ibid.*, pp. 109–10.
4 *Ibid.*, pp. 110–11. This essay on the relationship to T. S. Eliot was originally published in Hines (ed.), *The Composer's Point of View* (Norman, Okla., 1963), pp. 111–22; revised version published in Meirion Bowen (ed.), *Music of the Angels: Essays and Sketchbooks of Michael Tippett* (London, 1980), pp. 117–26. The 'Sketch for a Modern Oratorio' is published in both *Music of the Angels* and Bowen (ed.), *Tippett on Music*. Where any such duplication occurs the reference will be given to *Tippett on Music*.
5 Bowen (ed.), *Tippett on Music*, p. 114.
6 *Ibid.*, p. 115. For the presentation of these words in the sketch see *ibid.*, pp. 118–19. For the full revised text of the Owen quotation see C. Day Lewis (ed.), *The Collected Poems of Wilfred Owen* (London, 1963), p. 129.
7 Bowen (ed.), *Tippett on Music*, p. 115.
8 *Ibid.*, p. 122.
9 *Ibid.*, p. 123.
10 *Ibid.*, p. 114.
11 *Ibid.*, p. 160. The Owen lines are from the poem 'Strange Meeting'. See Day Lewis (ed.), *Collected Poems*, p. 35.
12 T. S. Eliot, *The Complete Poems and Plays* (London, 1969), p. 281.
13 Kemp, *Tippett*, p. 154.
14 Eliot, *The Complete Poems and Plays*, p. 97.
15 *Ibid.*, p. 243.

16 Bowen (ed.), *Tippett on Music*, p. 174; Eliot, *The Complete Poems and Plays*, p. 38.

17 Bowen (ed.), *Tippett on Music*, p. 175.

18 Eliot, *The Complete Poems and Plays*, p. 241.

19 Harriet Davidson, 'Improper Desire: reading *The Waste Land*', in A. David Moody (ed.), *The Cambridge Companion to T. S. Eliot* (Cambridge, 1994), p. 128.

20 For further consideration of this process see my 'Tippett's Second Symphony, Stravinsky and the Language of Neoclassicism: Towards a Critical Framework', in David Clarke (ed.), *Tippett Studies* (Cambridge, 1999), pp. 78–94.

21 Davidson, 'Reading *The Waste Land*', p. 128.

22 Jewel Spears Brooker, *Mastery and Escape: T. S. Eliot and the Dialectic of Modernism* (Amherst, Mass., 1994), p. 146.

23 Tippett, *Those Twentieth Century Blues*, pp. 62–3.

24 David Clarke, 'The Significance of the Concept "Image" in Tippett's Musical Thought: A Perspective from Jung', *Journal of the Royal Musical Association* 121 (1996), p. 83.

25 Bowen (ed.), *Tippett on Music*, p. 168.

26 *Collected works of C. G. Jung*, vol. ix/I, trans. R. F. C. Hull (London, 1959), pp. 17–18 (the italics are the translator's). As quoted in Bowen (ed.), *Tippett on Music*, p. 168.

27 Bowen (ed.), *Tippett on Music*, p. 128.

28 *Ibid.*, p. 129.

29 Anthony Stevens, *Jung* (Oxford, 1994), p. 47.

30 Kemp, *Tippett*, pp. 155–7.

31 Rainer Emig, *Modernism in Poetry: Motivations, Structures and Limits* (London, 1995), p. 61.

32 Arnold Whittall, 'Tippett and the Modernist Mainstream', in Geraint Lewis (ed.), *Michael Tippett OM: A Celebration* (Tunbridge Wells, Kent, 1985), p. 115.

33 Brooker, *Mastery and Escape*, p. 2.

34 The relationship between past and present within modernism has also become recognised in specific writings on modernism and music. According to Joseph Straus:

> The most important and characteristic musical works of the first half of this century incorporate and reinterpret elements of earlier music. This dual process, more than any specific element of style and structure, defines the mainstream of musical modernism.
>
> (Joseph Straus, *Remaking the Past: Musical Modernism and the Influence of the Tonal Tradition* (Cambridge, Mass., 1990), p. 2)

Although Straus restricts this description to the first half of the twentieth century, it is clearly possible to see the incorporation and reinterpretation of elements of earlier music as a crucial factor in Tippett's stylistic and technical development from *A Child of Our Time* onwards.

3 Origins

1 Tippett, *Those Twentieth Century Blues*, pp. 39–40.
2 *Ibid.*, p. 40.
3 Bowen (ed.), *Tippett on Music*, p. 111.
4 *Ibid.*, p. 182.
5 *Ibid.*, p. 112.
6 *Ibid.*
7 *Ibid.*
8 *Ibid.*, p. 132.
9 *Ibid.*, p. 148.
10 *Ibid.*, p. 166.
11 *Ibid.*, p. 176.

4 Synopsis – Analysis

1 Bowen (ed.), *Tippett on Music*, p. 63.
2 Kemp also draws attention to the tango characteristics of this accompaniment and provides an effective summary of Tippett's intentions: 'Here Tippett has deliberately used a tango rhythm (or at least the tango variant suggested by Weill in the "Zuhalterballade" of *Die Dreigroschenoper*), in order to evoke the familiar if in this case dispiriting sounds of popular music and thus set his tenor (the "ordinary man") in an immediately recognizable environment' (*Tippett*, p. 172).
3 *Ibid.*, p. 173 (Ex. 50).
4 Bowen, *Michael Tippett*, pp. 86–7.
5 Kemp, *Tippett*, p. 168 (Ex. 48).
6 *Ibid.*, p. 174.
7 *Ibid.*
8 *Ibid.*, pp. 174–5.

5 Musical Languages

1 James Weldon Johnson (ed.), *The Book of American Negro Spirituals* (London, 1926), pp. 37–8.

2 *Ibid.*, p. 50.

3 Bowen (ed.), *Tippett on Music*, p. 113.

4 Bowen, *Michael Tippett*, p. 90.

5 *Ibid.*, p. 90.

6 Bowen (ed.), *Tippett on Music*, p. 112. In his autobiography Tippett recollects the impact that the film *Green Pastures* made on him:

> The rightness of my choice [of spirituals] was confirmed when I saw *Green Pastures* – Marcus C. Connelly's marvellous film (made in 1936 with an all-black cast) – and heard the Hall Johnson Choir on the soundtrack singing spirituals in a free, bluesy manner. The scene in the film where Moses strikes dead Pharaoh's son and the succeeding spiritual, 'Go Down Moses', accompanied on the screen by the sight of feet tramping away, moved me deeply . . .
> (Tippett, *Those Twentieth Century Blues*, p. 50)

7 Bowen, *Michael Tippett*, p. 90.

8 Michael Tippett, *Moving into Aquarius* (London, 1974), pp. 92–3.

9 Bowen (ed.), *Tippett on Music*, p. 113.

10 Kemp, *Tippett*, p. 166.

11 The interpretation of the work as unified through these connections is also stated by Stuart Sillars:

> The spirituals are also united to the rest of the work by the way in which their frequent idioms become part of the melodic contours of its other movements. The minor third, flat seventh and open fifth which are characteristic of the spirituals' melodies are absorbed into other movements to give this further kind of unity. Most listeners are probably aware of this to an extent no greater than their awareness of the unifying intervallic progressions of a Brahms symphony, or the tone row of a Webern song, but they add to the music's organic unity and thus provide a major sense of growth and development through it.
> (Stuart Sillars, *British Romantic Art and the Second World War* (London, 1991), pp. 133–4)

12 Whittall, *The Music of Britten and Tippett*, p. 73.

13 Kemp, *Tippett*, p. 168.

14 *Ibid.*

15 Igor Stravinsky, *Poetics of Music*, trans. Arthur Knodel and Ingolf Dahl (Cambridge, Mass., 1947), pp. 36–7.

16 For another attempt to relate this statement to the music of Tippett see my 'Tippett's Second Symphony, Stravinsky and the Language of Neoclassicism', pp. 89–90.

17 Given the fundamental nature of the ambiguity which surrounds the tonal language of this work it is at times difficult to make any clear distinction between primary and secondary pitch relationships. However, even when the identification of a tonal centre and/or function is most inherently

problematic, the consistent sense of contextualised focus on specific pitches does provide for a salient status in relation to other pitch factors. For an overview of the theoretical problems involved in these issues see my 'Structure, Syntax and Style in the Music of Stravinsky', Ph.D. thesis, University of Exeter (1995), pp. 27–33.

18 Brooker, *Mastery and Escape*, p. 159. The reference is to James Frazer, *The Illustrated Golden Bough* (New York, 1978), a work to which Tippett himself has referred in several different contexts. However, it is notable that many Eliot scholars agree on the existence of some kind of background or framework to *The Waste Land* while differing as to its nature or identity. For example, in contrast to the view of Brooker, Harriet Davidson states that '*The Waste Land* can be read as a poem about the proper and the improper.' Davidson, 'Improper Desire', p. 122.

6 Reception

1 Bowen (ed.), *Tippett on Music*, p. 67. In his autobiography, Tippett again drew attention to Britten's enthusiasm for the work: 'At Oxted, Ben wanted to see what I had written and I produced *A Child of Our Time* from a drawer. He was very excited and said that it must be performed' (*Those Twentieth Century Blues*, p. 117).

2 John Amis, 'New Choral Work by Michael Tippett: A Child of Our Time', *The Musical Times* 85 (1944), p. 41.

3 Edwin Evans, 'A Child of Our Time', *The Musical Times* 85 (1944), p. 124.

4 William McNaught, review, *The Musical Times* 85 (1944), p. 144.

5 Eric Blom, review, *Music & Letters* 25 (1944), p. 124.

6 R.J. Manning, 'A Child of Our Time', *The Monthly Musical Record* 75 (1945), p. 179.

7 Colin Mason, 'Michael Tippett', *The Musical Times* 87 (1946), p. 140.

8 David Clarke, *Language, Form and Structure in the Music of Michael Tippett*, (New York and London, 1989), vol. I, p. 6.

9 Kemp, *Tippett*, p. 178.

10 Whittall, *The Music of Britten and Tippett*, p. 73.

11 *Merzbild* was a term invented by the artist Kurt Schwitters to describe his collages. Robert Hughes, following a description of Schwitters's techniques, provides the following explanation:

> Schwitters called them all 'Merz' paintings: the name was a fragment of a printed phrase advertising the Kommerz- und Privat-Bank, which had turned up in one of his collages. Their common theme was the city as compressor, intensifier of experience. So many people, and so many messages: so many

traces of intimate journeys, news, meetings, possession, rejection, with the city renewing its fabric of transaction every moment of the day and night, as a snake casts its skin, leaving the patterns of the lost epidermis behind as 'mere' rubbish.

12 Whittall, 'Tippett and the Modernist Mainstream', p. 113.

7 Legacy

1 Stephen Banfield, 'Vocal Music', in Banfield (ed.), *The Blackwell History of Music in Britain: The Twentieth Century* (Oxford, 1995), p. 420.
2 Whittall, *The Music of Britten and Tippett*, p. 216.
3 Brooker, *Mastery and Escape*, p. 140.
4 Whittall, *The Music of Britten and Tippett*, p. 216.
5 *Ibid.*, p. 217.
6 Bowen (ed.), *Tippett on Music*, p. 246.

Select bibliography

Banfield, Stephen (ed.). *The Blackwell History of Music in Britain: The Twentieth Century* (Oxford: Blackwell, 1995)

Bowen, Meirion. *Michael Tippett* (London: Robson, 1997)

Bowen, Meirion (ed.). *Music of the Angels: Essays and Sketchbooks of Michael Tippett* (London: Eulenburg, 1980)

Tippett on Music (Oxford: Clarendon Press, 1995)

Clarke, David. *Language, Form and Structure in the Music of Michael Tippett* (2 vols., New York and London: Garland, 1989)

'Tippett in and out of "Those Twentieth-Century Blues": The Context and Significance of an Autobiography', *Music & Letters* 74 (1993), pp. 399–411

'Visionary Images', *The Musical Times* 136 (1995), pp. 16–21

'The Significance of the Concept "Image" in Tippett's Musical Thought: A Perspective from Jung', *Journal of the Royal Musical Association* 121 (1996), pp. 82–104

Clarke, David (ed.). *Tippett Studies* (Cambridge: Cambridge University Press, 1999)

Eliot, T. S. *The Complete Poems and Plays* (London: Faber and Faber, 1969)

Kemp, Ian. *Tippett: The Composer and his Music* (London: Eulenburg, 1984)

Kemp, Ian (ed.). *Michael Tippett – A Symposium on his Sixtieth Birthday* (London: Faber, 1965)

Kermode, Frank (ed.). *Selected Prose of T. S. Eliot* (London: Faber and Faber, 1975)

Lewis, Geraint (ed.). *Michael Tippett OM: A Celebration* (Tunbridge Wells: The Baton Press, 1985)

Nicolosi, Robert J. 'T. S. Eliot and Music: An Introduction', *The Musical Quarterly* 66 (1980), pp. 192–204

Puffett, Derrick. 'The Fugue from Tippett's Second String Quartet', *Music Analysis* 5 (1986), pp. 233–64

'Tippett and the Retreat from Mythology', *The Musical Times* 136 (1995), pp. 6–14

Robinson, Suzanne. 'The Pattern from the Palimpsest: The Influence of T. S. Eliot on Michael Tippett', Ph.D. thesis, University of Melbourne (1990)

Sillars, Stuart. *British Romantic Art and the Second World War* (London: Macmillan, 1991)

Tippett, Michael. *Moving into Aquarius* (London: Routledge & Kegan Paul, 1959; reprinted with additional material London: Paladin, 1974)

White, Eric Walter. *Tippett and his Operas* (London: Barrie & Jenkins, 1979)

Whittall, Arnold. *Music Since the First World War* (London: Dent, 1977)

  Britten and Tippett: Studies in Themes and Techniques (Cambridge: Cambridge University Press, 1982,1990)

  'Resisting Tonality: Tippett, Beethoven and the Sarabande', *Music Analysis* 9 (1990), pp. 267–86

  'Acts of Renewal', *The Musical Times* 139 (1998), pp. 6–9

Index